Edexcel AS | UNIT 1

Economics

Competitive Markets:
How They Work and Why They Fail

Mark Gavin

330 GAV

Philip Allan Updates, an imprint of Hodder Education, part of Hachette Livre UK, Market Place, Deddington, Oxfordshire, OX15 0SE

Orders

Bookpoint Ltd, 130 Milton Park, Abingdon, Oxfordshire, OX14 4SB
tel: 01235 827720
fax: 01235 400454
e-mail: uk.orders@bookpoint.co.uk
Lines are open 9.00 a.m.–5.00 p.m., Monday to Saturday, with a 24-hour message answering service. You can also order through the Philip Allan Updates website: www.philipallan.co.uk

ISBN 978-0-340-94745-6

First printed 2008
Impression number 5 4 3 2 1
Year 2013 2012 2011 2010 2009 2008

This Guide has been written specifically to support students preparing for the Edexcel AS Economics Unit 1 examination. The content has been neither approved nor endorsed by Edexcel and remains the sole responsibility of the authors.

Typeset by Phoenix Photosetting, Chatham, Kent
Printed by MPG Books, Bodmin

Hachette Livre UK's policy is to use papers that are natural, renewable and recyclable products and made from wood grown in sustainable forests. The logging and manufacturing processes are expected to conform to the environmental regulations of the country of origin.

P1301

Contents

Introduction

■ ■ ■

Content Guidance

■ ■ ■

Questions and Answers

Supported multiple-choice questions

Data-response questions

Introduction

Aims

This guide has been written to prepare students for Unit 1 of Edexcel's Advanced Subsidiary (AS) GCE examination in economics. It provides an overview of the knowledge and skills required to achieve a high grade in the examination for Unit 1: Competitive Markets — How They Work and Why They Fail. This unit considers the nature of economics and examines how the price mechanism allocates resources in markets and why market failure may occur. It can be broken down into six topics that cover the unit specification:

(1) The nature of economics
(2) The demand for goods and services
(3) The supply of goods and services
(4) The determination of prices for goods and services and wage rates
(5) Market failure
(6) Government intervention to correct market failure

How to use this guide

This guide provides a summary of the knowledge and skills required to achieve a high grade in Unit 1. It also focuses on exam techniques, including typical questions and answers, and explains what the examiners are looking for. It should be used as a supplement for a taught course along with textbooks and other materials recommended by your teacher.

This introduction explains the examination format and the skills that will be tested. It also provides useful tips on revision planning and sitting the examination. A revision programme for a 4-week period before the Unit 1 examination is included.

The Content Guidance section provides an overview of the topics, identifying what has to be learnt and explaining key economic concepts and models. Typical examination mistakes made by students are also shown, plus links that exist between topics. These are favourite areas for the examiner to set questions on.

The final part of the guide provides questions and answers on the economic concepts and topics in Unit 1. There are four sets of 'supported multiple-choice questions', together with correct answers demonstrating maximum 4-mark responses.

Finally, there are four data-response questions covering relevant topics, with a selection of student answers ranging in quality from grade A to grade C. The examiner's comments that accompany these answers give an insight into how the marks are awarded and what pitfalls should be avoided.

Exam format

Unit 1 comprises 50% of the weighting for the AS examination (and 25% for the A-level). In the examination you are required to answer eight supported multiple-choice questions plus one data-response question from a choice of two.

The time allowed for the examination is 1 hour and 30 minutes. There are a maximum of 80 marks; 32 marks are available in the multiple-choice section and 48 marks in the data-response section of the exam paper. This means around 35 minutes should be spent on the multiple-choice section and 50 minutes on the data-response section, leaving 5 minutes to check and amend your work.

How to evaluate

Most candidates find 'evaluation' the most challenging part of the exam. Command words include *examine, evaluate, assess, discuss, comment upon* and *to what extent.* Any of these words in the question indicate that you should demonstrate some critical understanding of the issues being discussed.

As a strategy to gain evaluation marks in the examination, you should consider discussing one or more of the factors below where relevant to the question:

- **The advantages and disadvantages of an argument.** For example, if you are answering a question about the construction of more nuclear power stations to meet the UK's growing energy needs, you should consider the arguments and come to your own measured conclusion on whether more nuclear power plants should be built.
- **Prioritisation among factors.** For example, if you are asked about the causes of increasing house prices over the past 10 years, there are many factors which may have contributed to this and you should explain which ones are the most important.
- **The magnitude of an event or issue.** For example, if a question asks you about the effects of rising cocoa prices on the price of chocolate, this will depend on how much cocoa prices increase by and also the proportion of the cost of producing chocolate which is made up of cocoa. A 10% increase in cocoa prices may have relatively little effect on the price of chocolate, since it forms only a small proportion of total costs.
- **The short-run and long-run time periods.** For example, an increase in the price of wheat may have little impact on increasing the quantity supplied in the short run, since it takes farmers up to 9 months to grow the commodity. However, in the long run a high price will encourage farmers to allocate more of their land to growing wheat and so the quantity supplied could increase substantially.
- **The effect on consumers of the time period under consideration.** For example, an increase in mortgage interest rates may have little impact on house-holds with 2-year fixed interest rate mortgages, since the monthly repayments are likely to remain the same in the short run. However, once the 2-year period is up, households can expect an increase in the monthly interest repayments.

- **The quality of data.** For example, it may be helpful for more information to be provided in a data-response question to answer the question set. If you point out what further information you would need to answer the question more effectively or possible discrepancies in the data, then evaluation marks could be awarded.

The data-response questions and answers in this guide demonstrate how evaluation marks can be achieved in practice. Evaluation marks are only available in the data-response question for Unit 1.

A 4-week structured revision plan

Revision for AS and A2 examinations requires careful organisation and planning. A 4-week revision timetable that is useful to follow is shown here.

Days	Week 1	Week 2	Week 3	Week 4
1	Introductory economic concepts: positive and normative statements, scarcity, opportunity cost, production possibility frontiers.	Calculation of price elasticity of demand; the determinants of PED and the relationship with total revenue.	Definition and types of market failure; the relationship between private, external and social costs; diagrammatic explanation showing welfare loss.	Definition of public goods and reasons why they are unlikely to be provided in a free market economy.
2	Advantages and disadvantages of a free market economy. Advantages and disadvantages of the division of labour.	Calculation of income elasticity of demand; normal goods and inferior goods; calculation of cross elasticity of demand; substitutes and complementary goods.	The application of indirect taxes to internalise external costs and reach social optimum position; assess the use of the tax system in this way.	Immobility of labour (occupational and geographical); methods to reduce labour immobility.
3	Determinants of movements along, and shifts in, demand and supply curves.	Calculation of price elasticity of supply; the determinants of PES.	Advantages and disadvantages of other methods to solve external costs: tradable pollution permits, quotas, extension of property rights, regulation.	Unstable commodity markets and their impact on consumers and producers. Government intervention via minimum pricing and buffer stock programmes.

Days	Week 1	Week 2	Week 3	Week 4
4	Consumer and producer surplus; diagrammatic changes in their values. Functions of the price mechanism and market equilibrium.	Application of indirect taxes and subsidies to markets; the effects on consumers and producers.	The relationship between private, external and social benefits; diagrammatic explanation showing welfare gain; application of subsidies.	Definition of government failure; types of government failure.
5	Exam practice: complete one set of multiple-choice questions and one data-response question from this guide.	Exam practice: complete one set of multiple-choice questions and one data-response question from this guide.	Exam practice: complete one set of multiple-choice questions and one data-response question from this guide.	Exam practice: complete one set of multiple-choice questions and one data-response question from this guide.

How to answer supported multiple-choice questions

In Unit 1 there are eight supported multiple-choice questions which are worth 32 marks in total. For each question, 1 mark is awarded for selecting the correct answer and a further 3 marks can be gained for explanation. This means a maximum of 4 marks can be achieved per multiple-choice question.

If the incorrect option is selected, you can still achieve up to 3 marks for a relevant explanation. It is therefore always worth writing something, however unsure you are of the answer.

It is also possible to gain up to 2 marks by explaining why one or two of the alternative options are incorrect. This is a useful strategy to apply when uncertain about your explanation of the correct option or where your explanation lacks detail.

There are further guidance points, namely:
- **Keep in mind the time allocation.** You have 36 minutes to answer eight supported multiple-choice questions, or 4½ minutes per question. Do not spend too much time on any single question in the first instance as diminishing returns quickly set in.
- **Define the key economic concept in the question.** Usually 1 mark is available for an accurate definition of a key term in each supported multiple-choice question.
- **Be prepared to draw a diagram.** This can help improve your understanding and the quality of your explanation, especially in a unit which focuses on demand and supply analysis.
- **Be prepared to annotate any diagrams provided.** This might involve shading in areas of tax revenue, welfare loss, welfare gain, subsidy expenditure, consumer surplus or producer surplus, or shifting the production possibility frontier.

- **Answer all the questions.** It is surprising that some candidates do not even guess the answers to questions they do not understand. No marks are deducted for incorrect answers or explanations.
- **Consider working out the answer before looking at the options.** This can prevent distracters from confusing your thinking. After selecting your answer, you need to justify why it is correct, so think about the key economic model or concept underlying the question.
- **Eliminate impossible answers.** If you are able to eliminate three options then the final one, no matter how improbable, must be correct.
- **Learn from your mistakes.** When you get a question wrong or are unable to provide a proper explanation, you should find out what the correct response is. Supported multiple-choice questions are good indicators of your strengths and weaknesses in understanding particular topics.
- **Practice really does make perfect.** You should attempt as many past question papers as possible, including the ones in this guide. Often, past questions are re-worked into future questions.

How to answer data-response questions

In Unit 1, you have a choice between two data-response questions. It is important to spend several minutes considering both questions before choosing which one to answer. There are 48 marks available in the data-response question, which works out at approximately 1 minute per mark (around 50 minutes in total). The techniques involved in answering data-response questions are covered in more detail in the Unit 2 guide *Managing the Economy*. The key points are to make use of the information provided in your answer and to incorporate relevant economic concepts and models. Ensure you evaluate when required.

Content Guidance

Unit 1: Competitive Markets –– How They Work and Why They Fail is at the heart of economics. It is based on the market economy and how the price mechanism allocates resources between competing ends. Both product and labour markets are investigated. It also considers the causes of market failure, where the price mechanism fails to allocate resources efficiently. These are based on external costs and benefits, public goods, imperfect knowledge and unstable commodity markets. Government intervention to correct market failure and its effects are also investigated.

The price mechanism model has proved to be an effective tool for developing our understanding of the real world. It underpins all the other units in the Edexcel specification. In particular, the application of demand and supply analysis frequently appears in various guises: aggregate demand and aggregate supply in Units 2 and 4, market structures in Unit 3 (perfect competition, monopolistic competition, oligopoly and monopoly) and exchange rates and protectionism in Unit 4.

This section focuses on essential information for Unit 1:
- What is the nature of economics?
- What determines the demand for a good or service in a market?
- What determines the supply of a good or service in a market?
- What determines the price of a good or service in a market?
- How might a change in the price of a good or service be explained?
- What determines the wage rate for labour in a market?
- Why do some markets fail?
- How do governments attempt to correct market failure and what is government failure?

What is the nature of economics?

Essential information

Economics can be defined as the allocation of scarce resources to provide for unlimited human wants.

Scarcity

Scarcity arises because there are insufficient resources to provide for everyone's wants. It occurs in all economies, since resources are finite compared to human material wants. Scarcity is obvious in countries that face famine or drought, where insufficient food or water is available to meet everyone's needs. However, scarcity also exists in wealthy countries, since not all human material wants can be satisfied.

Scarcity means we have to make choices over the use of our limited resources to provide for our material wants. Some crucial decisions have to be made over what, how and for whom to produce. These decisions face consumers, producers and the government. Once a decision has been made over what to use a resource for, opportunity cost arises.

Opportunity cost

Opportunity cost refers to the value of the next best alternative which is forgone. Consumers, producers and government all face opportunity cost.

A consumer may have £20 available to spend on a meal at a restaurant or on the next best thing, which is a new t-shirt. The individual cannot buy both at the same time. If the consumer chooses to buy a meal then the opportunity cost is forgoing the new t-shirt.

A firm may have £50,000 available to invest in a new machine or to invest in a training programme for employees. The managers have to make a choice over the best use of the funds.

A government may have an extra £100 million of tax revenue. It might use this to build a new hospital but in doing so, forgoes the building of a large school, considered to be the next best alternative.

Types of resources

Resources, or **factors of production**, are inputs used in the production of goods and services. They are finite and can be classified into four types: land, labour, capital and enterprise.

Renewable and non-renewable resources

A **renewable resource** is one whose stock level can be maintained over a period of time. These include solar energy, wind power, water, oxygen, timber and soil.

However, renewable resources may decline over time if they are consumed at a faster rate than the environment can replenish them. They require careful management, to avoid such things as deforestation and soil erosion.

A **non-renewable resource** is one whose stock level is decreased over time as it is consumed. These resources include fossil fuels such as coal, oil and gas. They also include commodities such as steel, copper and aluminum. It is possible to reduce the rate of decline of non-renewable resources through recycling and the development of substitutes. The price mechanism also has a role to play in reducing the rate of consumption via higher prices.

Production possibility frontiers

A **production possibility frontier** shows the maximum potential level of output for two goods or services that an economy can achieve when all its resources are fully and efficiently employed, given the level of technology available. It can be used to illustrate scarcity and opportunity cost.

The diagram shows the production possibility frontier of an economy with capital and consumer goods. Initially, the economy is at point Z. To increase the production of capital goods by 20 units and move to point W, there is an opportunity cost of 30 units of consumer goods.

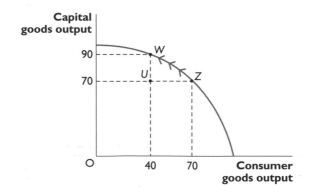

Production possibility frontier

The movement from Z to W increases the rate of economic growth, since capital goods are crucial for increasing production. Economic growth can be shown by an outward shift of the production possibility frontier. However, the loss of 30 units of consumer goods means that current living standards will fall in order to enable future living standards to rise at a faster rate.

If the economy is located at any point on its production possibility frontier, there is an efficient allocation of resources, since none are being wasted. However, if the economy is located within its production possibility frontier, there is an inefficient allocation of resources as not all are being used. At position U it is possible to increase production of both consumer and capital goods, by utilising unemployed resources. Since nothing is given up in return, there is no opportunity cost.

The shape of production possibility frontiers — curves and straight lines

A typical production possibility frontier is bowed to the origin and shows that, as more of one good is produced, an increasing amount of the other good is forgone. The opportunity cost rises. This is because not all resources are as efficient as other resources in the production of both goods. Diminishing returns set in.

A good example is the use of agricultural land in East Anglia and southwest England. We can assume that farm land can be used either for growing wheat or for livestock production. East Anglia has highly fertile and light soils with suitable rainfall for growing wheat. Output per acre is very high. However, as we move towards the south-west, the soil becomes too heavy and rainfall too high for growing wheat. Instead, livestock farming is far more productive per acre. If farmland in the southwest was converted to wheat production, yields would be very low and at a cost of forgoing considerable livestock output.

Shifts in the production possibility frontier

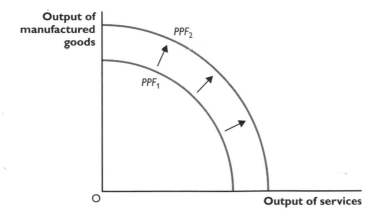

An increase in the production possibility frontier

A country's production potential may increase over time, which is shown in the diagram by an outward shift in its production possibility frontier. This represents economic growth and there are a number of possible causes: for example, an increase in the quantity or quality of resources; the expansion of further and higher education and government training schemes; or an increase in investment and development of new technology.

Occasionally the production possibility frontier may shift inwards towards the origin, indicating a decrease in the potential output of an economy. This may be caused by war or a natural disaster where many resources are destroyed. In 2004 the Tsunami devastated tourism and agriculture in some coastal areas of Thailand, reducing its productive capacity.

Specialisation and the division of labour

Specialisation occurs when an individual, a firm, a region or a country concentrates on the production of a limited range of goods and services. It has led to increases in productivity and living standards across the world. The UK specialises in the production of medicinal drugs, aircraft manufacture, tourism, and financial and business services. These goods and services can then be traded for other goods and services produced by other countries.

Specialisation can have disadvantages, notably when demand for a good or service falls, leading to a significant increase in unemployment. Also, a country specialising in the production and export of minerals may face problems of resource depletion.

The **division of labour** is one form of specialisation, where individuals concentrate on the production of a particular good or service. Production is broken down into a series of tasks, conducted by different workers. For example, house construction involves a range of specialist labour, including architects, surveyors, bricklayers, carpenters and electricians.

Advantages of the division of labour
- A person who spends time on one task quickly becomes highly skilled in it, e.g. a tyre fitter in a garage.
- No time is wasted in moving from one job to another, e.g. a packer on a sandwich production line.
- Capital equipment can be used continuously in production, e.g. the machinery on a motor vehicle production line.
- Less time is required to train workers for specific tasks.
- There is more choice of jobs for workers and they can specialise in tasks they are most suited to, e.g. a person who likes rock climbing might specialise in work as an outdoor pursuits leader.

These benefits lead to higher output per worker and thus help to reduce the cost per unit of output. Overall, living standards increase.

Disadvantages of the division of labour
- Repetition creates monotony and boredom. There could be a high turnover of staff, leading to increased recruitment and selection costs.
- Breaking down production into different tasks makes it easier to replace skilled workers with machines, leading to structural unemployment, e.g. motor vehicle welders being replaced by robots.
- Specialisation creates interdependence in production. If one group of workers goes on strike, it could halt production across the whole industry. For example, when train drivers call a 1-day stoppage, they disrupt the work of guards and ticket inspectors, as well as that of many commuters.

Free-market and mixed economies

An economy can be organised in different ways to produce goods and services. This ranges along a continuum from a free-market economy through to a mixed economy and then a centrally planned economy. The figure below shows the notion of a continuum.

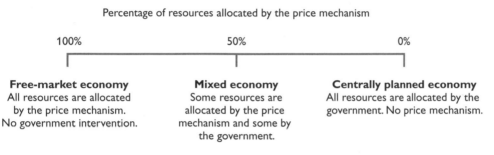

Percentage of resources allocated by the price mechanism

100%	50%	0%
Free-market economy	**Mixed economy**	**Centrally planned economy**
All resources are allocated by the price mechanism. No government intervention.	Some resources are allocated by the price mechanism and some by the government.	All resources are allocated by the government. No price mechanism.

Types of economic system

In reality, the vast majority of economies comprise a mixture of both private enterprise (the private sector) and state intervention (the public sector), thus being mixed economies. In the UK around 60% of resources are allocated by the private sector and 40% by the public sector. The government is a major provider of education, healthcare, defence and law and order in society. In other European economies (e.g. France, Germany and Sweden), the size of the public sector is greater, while in North America (the USA and Canada) it is lower. In all cases these are considered to be mixed economies.

A free-market economy

This is an economy where decisions on what, how and for whom to produce are left to the operation of the price mechanism. Resources are privately owned and economic decision making is decentralised among many individual consumers and producers. There is minimum government intervention.

There are no pure free-market economies in the world today since, in every economy, the government directly controls some resources and output. However, the proportion of government intervention tends to be significantly less in some developing countries, such as Malaysia and Thailand, compared to the developed world. Perhaps the best example of a developed country with a relatively small government sector is Japan.

A mixed economy

This is an economy where decisions on what, how and for whom to produce are made partly by the private sector and partly by the government. Most developed countries in the world today fall under this classification. Examples are the UK, France, Germany, Canada, Australia and Sweden.

The rationale of a mixed economy is to gain the advantages of the market economy while avoiding its disadvantages through government intervention. Often government intervention occurs to correct market failure: for example, the under-provision of merit goods such as education and healthcare or the non-provision of public goods such as defence. Government intervention usually arises to help markets work more effectively.

A centrally planned economy (command economy)

This is an economy where the government makes the decisions on what, how and for whom to produce. In a command economy the government has control of resources and economic decision making is centralised. There is no role for the price mechanism.

Positive and normative economics

Positive economics

Positive economics is concerned with facts and is value-free. It is a scientific approach to the discipline, where economists explain the outcome of a particular policy, but are not expected to take sides. Positive statements can be tested as true or false.

Normative economics

Normative economics is concerned with value-judgements and is a non-scientific approach to the discipline. A normative statement is an expression that something is right or wrong and so often includes the words *ought, should, fair, unfair, better* or *worse.*

Examination skills and concepts

- Using a production possibility frontier to explain the key concepts of opportunity cost, scarcity and unemployed resources.
- Understanding the causes of shifts in production possibility frontiers.
- Explaining how specialisation and the division of labour have increased output per head and living standards.
- Evaluating the economic arguments for and against a free-market economy.
- Familiarity with the concepts used in evaluating the performance of economic systems, e.g. efficiency, public goods, externalities, inflation, economic growth, unemployment, distribution of income and wealth, and the business cycle.
- Distinguishing between positive and normative statements in economics.

Common examination errors

- Incomplete definitions of key terms, such as production possibility frontier, opportunity cost and the division of labour.
- Confusing a reduction in cost per unit of output resulting from specialisation with a reduction in total costs of production.
- Developing a political rather than an economic argument in evaluating free-market and mixed economies.

- Listing the advantages and disadvantages of a free-market economy without evaluating the points when required by the question.
- Using the term 'opinion' rather than 'value-judgement' to explain normative economic statements.

Links with other topics Scarcity and opportunity costs are at the heart of economics and represent a way of thinking which runs through the whole specification. They link with all the other units:

- Economic growth (Unit 2)
- Productive and allocative efficiency (Unit 3)
- Conflicts between government macroeconomic aims (Unit 4)

What determines the demand for a good or service in a market?

Markets

A **market** is where buyers and sellers come into contact for the purpose of exchange. A price is agreed for exchange to take place. By price, we mean the exchange value of a good or service. There are many types of market and the Edexcel specification focuses on product, commodity and labour markets.

A product market refers to goods or services which the consumer derives utility from — they are wanted for their own sake. Examples are chocolate, wine and fast food.

A commodity market refers to raw materials or minerals used in the production of goods and services. Examples are wheat, sugar, oil and gold.

A labour market refers to the buying and selling of labour time for the production of goods and services. Examples include the markets for plumbers, teachers and accountants.

Demand

The buyers or consumers in a market are said to demand goods or services. **Demand** refers to the quantity of a good or service purchased at a given price over a given time period. Demand is different from just wanting a good or service. It is a want backed up by the ability to pay, which is also known as effective demand.

Downward-sloping demand curve

A **demand curve** is the quantity of a good or service that would be bought over a range of different price levels in a given period of time.

The demand curve slopes downwards from left to right for two reasons:

(1) The substitution effect. When the price of a good falls, it becomes cheaper relative to its substitutes and some consumers switch their purchases from more expensive substitutes to the good in question.

(2) The income effect. When the price of a good falls, the real income of a consumer may rise. In effect, the purchasing power of the consumer's nominal income has increased and so more of the good can be bought.

The market demand curve is the horizontal summation of each individual demand curve for a particular good or service.

Movement along a demand curve

There is a movement along a demand curve for a good *only* when there is a change in its price. A fall in price causes an **extension** in demand, and a rise in price causes a **contraction** in demand, as shown in the diagram below.

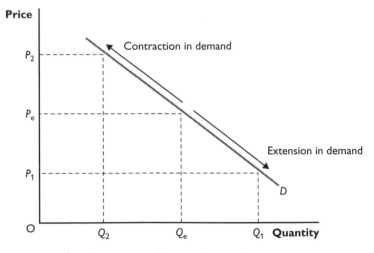

Movement along a demand curve

Shifts in the demand curve

An **increase** in demand refers to the whole demand curve shifting outwards to the right at every price level. A **decrease** in demand refers to the whole demand curve shifting inwards to the left at every price level.

There are various factors which can shift the demand curve for a good. For example, the demand for Sony PlayStation games consoles might increase due to:

- a fall in the price of complementary goods, such as computer games (Grand Theft Auto and Fifa Soccer)
- a rise in the price of substitute goods, such as the Microsoft Xbox 360 or the Nintendo Wii games consoles
- a change in fashion and tastes which make games consoles more popular as a leisure activity among young people
- increased advertising of PlayStation games and consoles
- an increase in real incomes (for normal goods) meaning that the PlayStation becomes more affordable for people to buy
- a decrease in income tax which leads to an increase in disposable income so that a PlayStation becomes more affordable
- an increase in the population or a change in the age structure of the population so that there are more teenagers likely to purchase a PlayStation
- an increase in credit facilities which make it easier to obtain funds to pay for a PlayStation games console

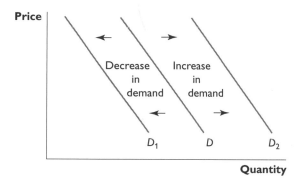

Shifts in demand curves

The diagram shows a decrease in demand by the shift of the demand curve leftwards to D_1 and an increase in demand is demonstrated by a rightward shift to D_2.

Price, income and cross elasticity of demand

Price elasticity of demand

Price elasticity of demand (PED) is the responsiveness in the demand for a good due to a change in its price. The formula to calculate it is:

$$\text{PED} = \frac{\text{percentage change in quantity demanded of good A}}{\text{percentage change in price of good A}}$$

In most circumstances, a minus answer is obtained, indicating that the two variables of price and demand move in opposite directions. There is a negative gradient.

Types of price elasticity of demand

If PED is greater than 1, the good is price elastic: that is, the percentage change in demand is greater that the percentage change in price. For example, a 10% rise in the price of holidays to Florida may cause a 20% decrease in the quantity demanded; PED is –2.

If PED is less than 1, the good is price inelastic: that is, the percentage change in demand is less than the percentage change in price. For example, a 10% fall in price of coffee may cause a 5% increase in the quantity demanded; PED is –0.5.

If PED is equal to 1, the good has unit elasticity: that is, the percentage change in demand is the same as the percentage change in price. For example, a 10% fall in the price of apples may cause a 10% rise in the quantity demanded; PED is –1.

If PED is equal to zero, the good is perfectly inelastic: that is, a change in price has no effect on the quantity demanded. The demand curve is vertical. An example might be heroin to a drug addict.

If PED is infinite, the good is perfectly elastic: that is, a rise in price causes demand to fall to zero. The demand curve is horizontal.

The demand curves below show the different elasticities.

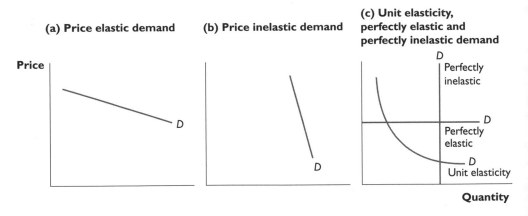

Different price elasticities of demand

The relationship between price elasticity of demand and total revenue
Elasticity varies along a straight-line demand curve, as shown in the following diagram. Elasticity falls as you move along the curve from the top left to the bottom right. At the mid-point, demand has unit elasticity.

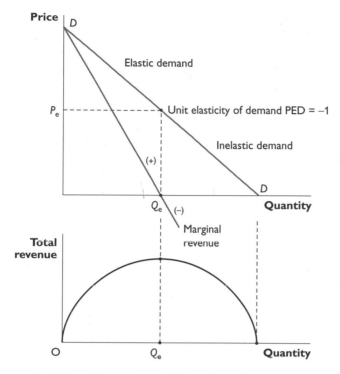

Relationship between PED and total revenue

Total revenue

Total revenue refers to the total payments a firm receives from selling a given quantity of goods or services. It is the price per unit of a good multiplied by the quantity sold. The total revenue a firm receives from selling a good will be equal to the total spending by consumers on that good.

A firm's **total revenue will increase** as long as **price is moving towards the mid-position of the demand curve** (where there is **unit elasticity**). It is important for firms to know the PED of their output when making pricing decisions, because this affects revenue and profitability.

If demand is elastic, then a cut in price increases total consumer spending and hence revenue to the firm. On the other hand, a rise in price causes total consumer spending to fall and so firms lose revenue.

If demand is inelastic, then an increase in price increases total consumer spending and hence revenue to the firm. On the other hand, a fall in price causes total consumer spending to fall and so firms lose revenue.

Once unit price elasticity has been reached, the firm is maximising its total revenue. Note the relationship between PED and marginal revenue, which falls during a move down the demand curve. As long as marginal revenue is positive, demand is price elastic. When marginal revenue is zero, demand is unit elastic; when marginal revenue is negative, demand is inelastic.

Determinants of price elasticity of demand

- **Availability of substitutes.** The more narrowly a good is defined, the more substitutes it tends to have and so its demand is elastic. For example, cod, a type of fish, has many substitutes such as plaice, rock, salmon and haddock. However, the more broadly a good is defined, the fewer substitutes it tends to have and so demand is less elastic. For example, there are few close substitutes for fish as a whole and so demand tends to be relatively less elastic.
- **Luxury and necessity goods.** Luxury goods, such as racing cars and caviar, tend to have an elastic demand, whereas necessity goods, like bread and underwear, tend to have an inelastic demand.
- **Proportion of income spent on the good.** If a high percentage of income is spent on the good, as with a new car or boat, demand tends to be price elastic. However, for goods that take up a small percentage of income, such as newspapers and tomato sauce, demand will tend to be price inelastic.
- **Addictive and habit-forming goods.** Tobacco, alcohol and coffee are the type of goods that tend to be price inelastic in demand.
- **The time period**. For most goods demand is less elastic in the short run than in the long run. For example, a rise in the price of household electricity is likely to have only a minor effect on consumption in the short run. In the long run, households can cut back on consumption by switching to gas for their cooking and heating. This means demand eventually becomes more responsive to changes in price.

Income elasticity of demand

Income elasticity of demand (YED) is the responsiveness of demand for a good or service to a change in real income. (Real income refers to the spending power of money income — the amount of goods and services which can be purchased with one's nominal income.) The formula to calculate YED is:

$$YED = \frac{\text{percentage change in demand for a good}}{\text{percentage change in real income}}$$

Normal goods

In most circumstances YED is positive which means the two variables of income and demand move in the same direction. In other words, a rise in income causes a rise in quantity demanded.

Inferior goods

Occasionally, YED is negative which means the two variables of income and demand move in opposite directions. This is because people tend to demand higher-quality goods as their incomes rise, substituting them for lower-quality products. The next diagram shows the demand curve for an inferior good compared with that of a normal good in relation to income.

(a) Normal good

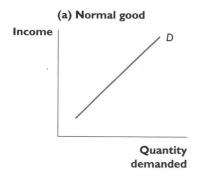

(b) Inferior good

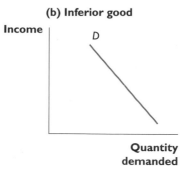

Income elasticity of demand

Luxury Good ≥1

Necessaty goods 0 to 1

Cross elasticity of demand

Cross elasticity of demand (XED) is the responsiveness of demand for good B to a change in price of good A. The formula to calculate XED is:

$$XED = \frac{\text{percentage change in demand for good B}}{\text{percentage change in price of good A}}$$

Cross elasticity of demand is used to determine whether goods are complements or substitutes for each other.

Substitute goods

Substitute goods are in competitive demand. For example, a rise in the price of coffee may cause an increase in demand for tea. XED is positive for substitute goods, as the two variables of price and demand move in the same direction. There is a positive gradient.

Complementary goods

Complementary goods are in joint demand. They tend to be consumed together. For example, a fall in the price of tennis rackets may cause an increase in demand for tennis balls. XED is negative for complementary goods, as the two variables of price and demand move in opposite directions. There is a negative gradient.

Note: a cross elasticity of demand of zero means there is no relationship between two goods, such as chocolate and beef.

The following diagram demonstrates cross elasticity of demand for complementary goods and substitute goods.

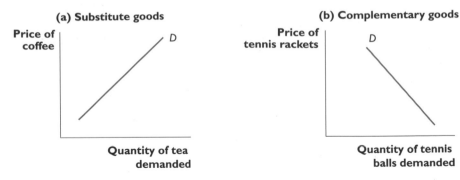

Cross elasticity of demand

Examination skills and concepts

- Distinguishing between a movement along and shifts in a demand curve.
- Identifying the factors that may shift the demand curve.
- Calculating price, income and cross elasticity of demand.
- Understanding the meaning of (+) and (−) answers to elasticity calculations.
- Rearranging the elasticity formula in order to calculate the percentage change in a variable.
- Calculating the original, the change in or new level of total revenue from data on price elasticity of demand.
- Distinguishing between inelastic and elastic demand curves.
- Distinguishing between normal goods and inferior goods.
- Distinguishing between complementary goods and substitute goods.
- Explaining the determinants of price elasticity of demand.
- Explaining the significance of elasticity of demand to consumers, producers and the government.

Common examination errors

- Confusion between movements along and shifts in the demand curve.
- Confusing the determinants of price elasticity of demand and price elasticity of supply.
- Confusing elasticity with the gradient of a demand curve. Straight-line demand curves have constant gradients but different elasticities along them.
- Using an incorrect formula for elasticity, with the price and quantity variables placed the wrong way round.
- Placing the decimal point in the wrong position when calculating elasticity.
- Failing to put the minus or plus signs into answers. This often leads to candidates confusing normal goods with inferior goods.
- Confusion over how to work out percentages and percentage change in variables.
- Confusion over the relationship between price elasticity of demand and total revenue.

Links with other topics Demand and elasticity are extremely important concepts which link with many other topics in the specification:
- Price elasticity of demand in different market structures, price discrimination, operation of cartels and pricing strategies (Unit 3).
- The incidence of indirect taxation and subsidies (Unit 1).
- Aggregate demand (Unit 2).
- Commodity markets and government intervention via buffer stock schemes and minimum prices (Unit 1).
- Labour markets and the national minimum wage (Unit 1).
- Exchange rates and the effects of depreciation or appreciation of currency on the balance of payments (Unit 4).

What determines the supply of a good or service in a market?

Supply

The sellers or producers in a market are said to supply goods and services. **Supply** refers to the quantity of a good or service that firms are willing to sell at a given price and over a given period of time.

An upward-sloping supply curve

A **supply curve** is the quantity of a good or service that firms are willing to sell to a market over a range of different price levels in a given period of time. The supply curve slopes upwards from left to right for two reasons:

(1) As price rises, it encourages firms to supply more of a good to make more profit.

(2) As firms raise output in the short run, they face rising production costs. To cover the rising costs, firms need to be able to charge higher prices to consumers. Higher prices can enable marginal firms to enter a market.

The market supply curve is the horizontal summation of individual firms' supply curves for a particular good or service.

Movement along a supply curve

There is movement along a supply curve for a good *only* when there is a change in its price. A rise in price causes an **extension** in supply, and a fall in price causes a **contraction** in supply, as shown in the next diagram.

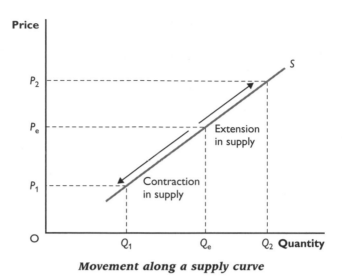

Movement along a supply curve

Shifts in the supply curve

An **increase** in supply refers to the whole supply curve shifting outwards to the right at every price level (to S_2 in the diagram below). A **decrease** in supply refers to the whole supply curve shifting inwards to the left at every level (to S_1 in the diagram).

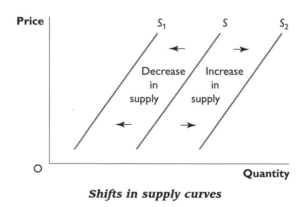

Shifts in supply curves

There are various factors that can shift the supply curve of a good. For example, the supply of oil could increase due to:

- improvements in technology, e.g. the extraction of oil from more difficult places (under the sea bed in deeper water)
- a reduction in labour costs, e.g. lower wages for oil platform and oil refinery workers
- a reduction in capital costs, e.g. oil platforms, pipelines and refineries
- a reduction in transport costs, e.g. an increase in size of oil tankers

- discovery of new oil fields, e.g in the Falklands
- an increase in the number of firms in the oil industry
- a decrease in the market influences of OPEC (Organisation of Petroleum Exporting Countries), a producer cartel. (This may occur if individual member states decide to produce more than the agreed oil quotas.)
- good weather making it easier to extract oil from Alaska or under the sea bed
- a reduction in indirect taxation on oil
- an increase in government subsidies to oil producers

Price elasticity of supply

Price elasticity of supply (PES) is the responsiveness of the supply of a good to a change in its price. The formula to calculate PES is:

$$\text{PES} = \frac{\text{percentage change in supply of a good}}{\text{percentage change in price of a good}}$$

In most cases a positive answer is obtained, indicating that the two variables of price and quantity move in the same direction. There is a positive gradient.

If PES is greater than 1, the good is price elastic: that is, the percentage change in supply is greater than the percentage change in price of the good.

If PES is less than 1, the good is price inelastic: that is, the percentage change in supply is less than the percentage change in price of the good.

If PES is equal to 1, the good is unit elastic: that is, the percentage change in supply is the same as the percentage change in price of the good.

If PES is equal to zero, the good is perfectly inelastic: that is, a change in price has no effect on the quantity supplied. The supply curve is vertical.

If PES is infinite, the good is perfectly elastic. The supply curve is horizontal.

The diagrams below show the different price elasticities of supply.

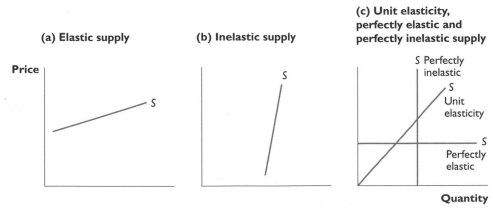

Different price elasticities of supply

Determinants of price elasticity of supply

- **Level of spare capacity.** A high level of spare capacity in a firm means that it can raise production quickly, so supply tends to be elastic. A firm or industry operating at full capacity is unable to raise output quickly and so supply tends to be inelastic.

- **The state of the economy.** In a recession there are many unemployed resources and so there is a high level of spare capacity. Firms find it relatively easy to raise supply if needed.

- **Level of stocks of finished goods in a firm.** A high level of stocks means that the firm can increase supply quickly, so supply is elastic: for example, US motor vehicle manufacturers often have stockpiles of cars waiting to sell. Alternatively, a firm or industry operating with low stocks is unable to raise output quickly and so supply tends to be inelastic. This is more likely to be the case for a firm making designer wedding dresses.

- **Perishability of the product.** Some goods cannot be stockpiled: for example, some agricultural goods such as fresh fruit, vegetables and flowers are highly perishable. These goods are typically inelastic in supply. On the other hand, manufactured goods tend to be non-perishable and so can be stockpiled by firms in order to meet anticipated increases in demand. Examples are household electrical goods such as fridges, freezers and washing machines.

- **The ease of entry to an industry.** If there are high entry barriers to an industry then it will be difficult for new firms to enter, even with the attraction of high prices and profits. Sometimes existing producers deliberately create entry barriers, so supply may be restricted and inelastic.

- **The time period under consideration.** This is perhaps the most important determinant of elasticity of supply. The **short run** is the period of time in which a firm is able to increase supply with its existing capacity. At least one factor input is likely to be fixed in quantity in the short run, which makes it difficult for a firm to raise production. Supply tends to be relatively inelastic. The **long run** is the period of time in which a firm is able to increase supply by adding to its production capacity. All factor inputs are variable in the long run, making it easier for a firm to raise production. Supply tends to be relatively elastic.

For many agricultural products, supply is inelastic in the short run because the output from the summer and autumn harvests depends on the amount of seed planted at the start of the year. It takes an even longer period of time to raise the supply of dairy products such as milk and beef because these depend on the nurturing of animals over several years.

The supply of minerals may also be inelastic in the short run due to the length of time required to explore and discover new deposits and then extract them. The costs and technical complexities involved could be phenomenal: for example, developing a new iron ore mine in Western Australia to cater for increasing demand from China. This will require heavy machinery and the construction of new rail and road links.

Examination skills and concepts

- Distinguishing between a movement along and shifts in a supply curve.
- Identifying the factors that may shift the supply curve.
- Calculating price elasticity of supply.
- Rearranging the elasticity formula in order to calculate the percentage change in a variable.
- Distinguishing between inelastic and elastic supply curves.
- Explaining the determinants of price elasticity of supply, especially the importance of time.
- Explaining the significance of elasticity of supply to consumers, producers and the government.

Common examination errors

- Confusing movements along and shifts in the supply curve.
- Confusing the determinants of price elasticity of supply and price elasticity of demand.
- Confusing elasticity with the gradient of a supply curve. Straight-line supply curves have constant gradients but different elasticities along them.
- Using an incorrect formula for elasticity, with the price and quantity variables placed the wrong way round.
- Placing the decimal point in the wrong position when calculating elasticity.
- Failing to define the terms 'elastic' and 'inelastic' supply.
- Confusion over how to work out percentages and percentage changes in variables.

Links with other topics
Supply and elasticity are extremely important concepts which link with many other topics in the specification:

- The determination of equilibrium price and quantity for a good or service (Unit 1).
- Derivation of marginal cost curves under perfect competition (Unit 3).
- The incidence of indirect taxation and subsidies (Unit 1).
- Producer surplus (Unit 1).
- Aggregate supply (Unit 2), short-run and long-run aggregate supply curves (Unit 4).
- Commodity markets and government intervention via buffer stock schemes and minimum prices (Unit 1).
- Labour markets and the national minimum wage (Unit 1).

What determines the price of a good or service in a market?

Equilibrium in a market

Equilibrium means there is a balance in the market, with no tendency for price or output to change. The equilibrium price and quantity of a good are obtained from the point of intersection between the demand and supply curves. In the table and figure below, the equilibrium price is £80 per unit and the quantity is 30 units per week.

Price	Quantity demanded per week	Quantity supplied per week
£100	10	50
£90	20	40
£80	30	30
£70	40	20
£60	50	10

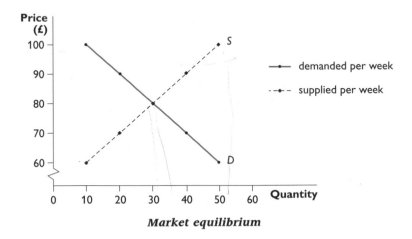

Market equilibrium

Excess supply and excess demand

In a free market, price cannot remain above or below the equilibrium position for long. For example, at a price of £100 there is an **excess supply** of 40 units. In order to sell the surplus, producers tend to reduce price and this encourages consumers to buy more. Demand extends and supply contracts until the equilibrium price of £80 is reached.

At a price of £60 there is an **excess demand** of 40 units. Consumers tend to bid up the price in order to obtain the good and this encourages producers to supply more. Supply extends and demand contracts until the equilibrium price of £80 is reached. Thus, the price mechanism automatically eliminates surpluses and shortages of a good, something that Adam Smith referred to as the 'invisible hand' of the market.

Consumer and producer surplus

Consumer surplus is the extra amount of money consumers are prepared to pay for a good or service above what they actually pay. It is the utility or satisfaction gained from a good or service in excess of that paid for it.

Producer surplus is the extra amount of money paid to producers above what they are willing to accept to supply a good or service. It is the extra earnings obtained by a producer above the minimum required to supply the good or service.

The areas of consumer and producer surplus are shown in the diagram. Consumer surplus is the area above the equilibrium price but below the demand curve; producer surplus is the area below the equilibrium price and above the supply curve.

Note that a shift in the demand or supply curve, leading to a new market price, will cause the amount of both consumer and producer surplus to change.

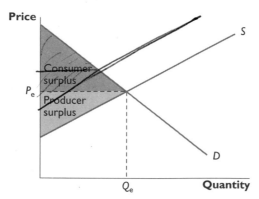

Consumer surplus and producer surplus

Functions of the price mechanism

Price is the exchange value of a good or service. The **price mechanism** refers to the way price responds to changes in demand or supply for a product or factor input, so that a new equilibrium position is reached in a market. It is the principal method of allocating resources in a market economy. The price mechanism has several functions:

- **A rationing device.** Resources are scarce, which means that the goods and services produced from them are limited in supply. The price mechanism allocates these goods and services to those who are prepared to pay the most for them. In effect, price will rise or fall until equilibrium is reached between the quantity demanded and quantity supplied.

- **An incentive device.** Rising prices tend to act as an incentive to firms to produce more of a good or service, since higher profits can be earned. Rising prices also mean firms are able to cover the extra costs involved with increasing output.
- **A signalling device.** The price mechanism indicates changes in the conditions of demand or supply. For example, an increase in demand for a good or service raises its price and encourages firms to expand their supply, while a decrease in demand lowers the price and causes firms to contract their supply. Consequently, more or fewer resources are allocated to the production of a particular good or service.

How might a change in the price of a good or service be explained?

Any of the factors which may shift demand or supply curves will lead to a change in price of a good or service. The role of indirect taxes and subsidies in influencing price is now considered in more detail.

Indirect taxes

A tax is a compulsory charge made by the government, on goods, services, incomes or capital. The purpose is to raise funds to pay for government spending programmes. There are two types of tax: direct and indirect.

A **direct tax** is levied directly on an individual or organisation. Direct taxes are generally paid on incomes: for example, personal income tax and corporation tax (on company profits).

An **indirect tax** is usually levied on the purchase of goods and services. It represents a tax on expenditure. There are two types of indirect tax: specific and *ad valorem* taxes. A specific tax is charged as a fixed amount per unit of a good, such as a litre of wine or a packet of cigarettes. An excise tax is a good example. An *ad valorem* tax is charged as a percentage of the price of a good: for example, VAT of 17.5% is added on to restaurant meals.

The imposition of an indirect tax raises the price of a good or service. The tax is added to the supply price, effectively causing the supply curve to shift vertically upwards and to the left (a decrease in supply). A **specific tax** causes a parallel shift of the supply curve to the left, as shown in part (a) of the following diagram. An *ad valorem* **tax** causes a pivotal rotation of the supply curve to the left, as shown in part (b).

(a) Specific tax

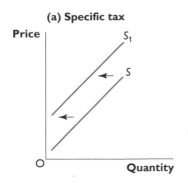

(b) *Ad valorem* tax

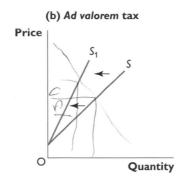

The incidence of an indirect tax

The tax incidence usually falls partly on consumers and partly on producers, depending on the relative price elasticities of demand and supply for the good or service. A combination of price inelastic demand and price elastic supply tends to place most of the tax burden on consumers; addictive goods such as tobacco and alcohol tend to be price inelastic in demand. This means that firms are able to pass most of the burden of tax on to consumers via higher prices.

However, a combination of price elastic demand and price inelastic supply tends to place most of the tax burden on the producers. It may also lead to a significant reduction in output and employment. Consequently, a government may be reluctant to place high indirect taxes on these types of goods or services.

The figure below shows the effects of a specific tax on a good that is price inelastic in demand. Before the tax, equilibrium price is P_e and quantity Q_e. After the tax is imposed, the supply curve shifts to S_1 and the equilibrium price rises to P_1 while quantity falls to Q_1. The total tax area is $XYWP_1$.

The incidence of tax paid by consumers is shown by the actual rise in market price from P_e to P_1. Consumers pay the amount of tax shown by the area XZP_eP_1. The tax paid by producers is the remaining area $ZYWP_e$.

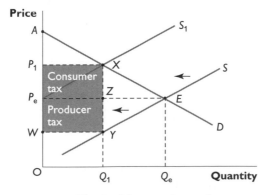

The incidence of taxation

Subsidies

A **subsidy** is a grant, usually provided by the government, to encourage suppliers to increase production of a good or service, leading to a fall in its price. Bus and train companies are often given subsidies in order to increase the number of bus and train services, which benefits both the firms and consumers.

A subsidy is often paid directly to producers, but as they respond by increasing output, the market price falls and this indirectly passes on some of the gain to consumers. If demand is price inelastic, then the market price falls by a relatively large amount, increasing the benefits to consumers. If demand is price elastic, then market price falls by a relatively small amount and so there is less gain for consumers. The diagram below shows the imposition of a government subsidy for a good.

Before the subsidy, equilibrium price is P_e and Q_e. After the subsidy is imposed, the supply curve shifts to S_2 and equilibrium price falls to P_2 while the quantity rises to Q_2. The total subsidy area is $RLGP_2$.

The amount of subsidy that consumers gain is shown by the actual fall in market price from P_e to P_2. They gain by paying a lower price for the good. The consumer subsidy area is RTP_eP_2. The remaining subsidy area of $TLGP_e$ represents the gain made by producers.

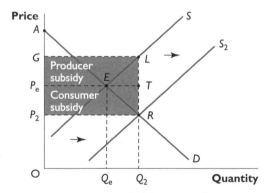

A government subsidy to producers

What determines the wage rate in a labour market?

In a competitive labour market the wage rate is determined by the interaction of demand and supply. The demand for labour is undertaken by firms, which require workers to help produce goods and services. The supply of labour comes from the general population and, in particular, the workforce of an economy.

In practice there are many different types of labour market: for example, shop assistants, kitchen chefs and lawyers. Labour markets also include public sector workers where the government is a major employer of labour: for example, teachers, nurses and police officers.

The demand for labour

The demand for labour is a **derived demand**. It is derived from the demand for the goods and services it makes. For example, the demand for building workers is derived from the demand for new housing.

The figure below shows how an increase in demand for new housing will cause an increase in demand for building workers, such as bricklayers and carpenters. The effect is to increase the wage rate from W_e to W_1 and the quantity employed from N_e to N_1.

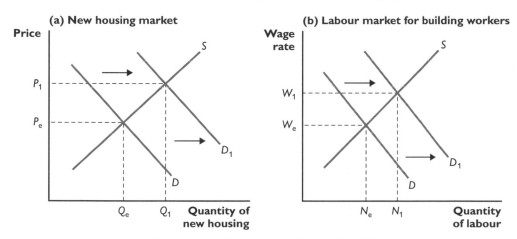

An increase in demand for new housing and building workers

There are several key determinants of the demand for labour:
- **Demand for the final product.** An increase in demand for a good or service is likely to cause an increase in demand for the labour involved in making it. Firms have a profit incentive, if demand and prices increase, to supply more of a good or service.
- **The wage rate.** A fall in the wage rate means that labour becomes more affordable and so firms are likely to demand more labour.
- **Other labour costs.** For example, a fall in employers' national insurance contributions on behalf of their staff is likely to raise the quantity demanded.
- **Price of other factor inputs.** An increase in the price of capital might encourage firms to employ more labour and cut back on the use of machinery and equipment where possible. This is because labour and capital may be substitutes in the production process.
- **Productivity of labour.** An increase in output per worker may lead to higher revenue and profits, encouraging firms to employ more people.

- **Government employment regulations.** The fewer the number of regulations, the greater the demand for labour is likely to be. For example, if it becomes easy to hire and fire staff or to change working conditions, then the increased labour flexibility may encourage firms to employ more people. However, a national minimum wage (NMW) set above the free-market wage may cause a decrease in the quantity of labour demanded.

The supply of labour

This refers to the quantity and quality of labour hours offered for work over a given time period. There are various factors which determine the supply of labour, namely:

- **The wage rate.** An increase in the wage rate will encourage more people to offer their services for work. A higher wage rate means the opportunity cost of leisure time increases, encouraging people to work longer hours.
- **Other net advantages of work.** Improvements in working conditions will also tend to increase the supply of labour: for example, a good pension, paid holidays, job security and promotion prospects.
- **Net migration.** Over recent years the UK has experienced a significant increase in immigration from central and eastern Europe, helping to boost the economy.
- **Income tax.** A reduction in income tax will increase disposable incomes and so offer a greater incentive for people to work. Many people will substitute work for leisure time, increasing the supply of labour.
- **Benefit reform.** A reduction in benefits (e.g. incapacity benefit, housing benefit and the jobseeker's allowance) may provide a greater incentive for people to look for work and so increase the supply of labour.
- **Trade unions.** Trade unions act to increase wage rates and improve other working conditions through collective bargaining with employers. This may encourage an increase in the supply of labour.
- **Government regulations.** An increase in employment protection or the intro-duction of a national minimum wage will tend to improve working conditions and so increase the supply of labour. However, it is also possible that government regulations reduce the supply of labour (for example, the EU Work Time Directive limits the maximum hours of work per week to 48 for most employees).
- **Social trends.** There has been a significant increase in the number of women in the workforce over the past 40 years. This reflects an improvement in equal oppor-tunities, childcare facilities and social attitudes.

Examination skills and concepts

- Drawing a demand and supply diagram to show equilibrium price and quantity.
- Explaining the meaning of excess demand and excess supply.
- Distinguishing between movement along and shifts in demand and supply curves.
- Drawing a diagram to show increases and decreases in demand.
- Drawing a diagram to show increases and decreases in supply.
- Drawing a diagram to show the areas of consumer surplus and producer surplus.

- Applying the factors that can cause shifts in demand and supply curves to various markets.
- Drawing a diagram to show the effects of an indirect tax and to identify the areas of consumer and producer tax.
- Drawing a diagram to show the effects of a subsidy and to identify the areas of consumer and producer subsidy.
- Being able to calculate the total tax area and subsidy area by use of tabular data, rather than diagrams.
- Drawing a diagram to show the effects of a national minimum wage.

Common examination errors

- Confusion between excess demand and excess supply.
- Failing to label a demand and supply diagram properly or to integrate it into the text.
- Incomplete definitions of consumer surplus and producer surplus.
- Incorrect drawing of the tax area following the imposition of an indirect tax on a good.
- Confusion of consumer tax area and producer tax area.
- Incorrect drawing of the subsidy area following the imposition of a subsidy on a good.
- Confusion of consumer subsidy area and producer subsidy area.

Links with other topics The price mechanism permeates the whole specification and you can expect to apply the model to any of the units. There are strong links with the following topics:

- Elasticity (Unit 1).
- External costs and benefits (Unit 1).
- Aggregate demand and aggregate supply curves, supply-side and demand-side policies (Unit 2).
- Foreign currency markets (Unit 4).

Why do some markets fail?

Market failure occurs when the price mechanism causes an inefficient allocation of resources; the forces of demand and supply lead to a net welfare loss in society. Consequently, resources are not allocated to their best or optimum use.

There are various types of market failure and you may come across different classifications in your textbooks. However, the Edexcel Unit 1 specification focuses on the following: externalities, public goods, imperfect market information, labour immobility and unstable commodity markets.

Externalities

Externalities are those costs or benefits which are external to an exchange. They are third party effects ignored by the price mechanism.

Externalities are also known as *indirect costs* and *benefits*, or as *spillovers from production* or *consumption* of a good or service. In effect, external costs are *negative externalities* and external benefits are *positive externalities*.

External costs

External costs may occur in the production and the consumption of a good or service. An example of an external cost in production is a chemical firm polluting a river with its waste. This causes an external cost to the fishing and water supply industries. Fish catches may be reduced and it may become very expensive to purify water to meet the European Commission's safety standards.

An example of an external cost in consumption is a person smoking tobacco, polluting the air for others. The effect is to cause passive smoking, where non-smokers may suffer the same illnesses as smokers.

Private costs

In a free market, producers are only concerned with the private costs of production. These are costs internal to the firm, which it directly pays for. These costs include wages for workers, rent of buildings, payment for raw materials, machinery costs, electricity and gas costs, insurance, packaging and transport costs from running lorries. Private costs may also refer to the market price that a consumer pays for a good or service.

Social costs

By adding private costs to external costs we obtain social costs. This means that external costs are the difference between private costs and social costs. The marginal private cost and marginal social cost curves often diverge, indicating that external costs increase disproportionately with output. However, it is possible that external costs per unit of output remain constant, in which case the marginal private cost and marginal social cost curves are drawn parallel to each other. The relationship between private cost, external cost and social cost is shown below.

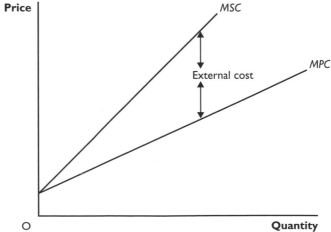

The relationship between private cost, external cost and social cost in the production of a good

Note that the Edexcel specification focuses on diagrammatic analysis of external costs in production.

External benefits

External benefits may occur in the production and consumption of a good or service. An example of an external benefit in production is the recycling of waste materials such as newspapers, glass and tins. It has the benefit of reducing the amount of waste disposal for landfill sites as well as re-using materials for production. It helps to promote sustainable economic growth.

An external benefit in consumption is the vaccination of an individual against various diseases. It reduces the possibility of other people catching a disease who come into contact with the vaccinated individual.

Private benefits

In a free market, consumers are only concerned with the private benefits or utility from consuming a good or service. Economists assume this can be measured by the price that consumers are prepared to pay for a good or service. Private benefits may also refer to the revenue that a firm obtains from selling a good or service.

Social benefits

By adding private benefits to external benefits we obtain social benefits. This means external benefits are the difference between private benefits and social benefits. The marginal private benefit and marginal social benefit curves often diverge, indicating that external benefits increase disproportionately with output consumed, as shown in the diagram. However, it is possible that external benefit per unit consumed will remain constant, in which case the marginal private benefit and marginal social benefit curves are drawn parallel to each other.

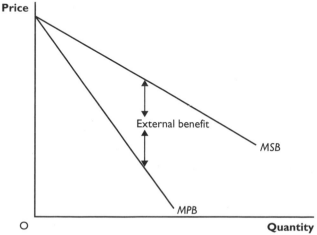

The private benefits, external benefits and social benefits from the consumption of a good

Note that the Edexcel specification focuses on diagrammatic analysis of external benefits in consumption of goods and services.

The free-market equilibrium

The supply curve for a firm is the marginal private cost curve (*MPC*). The addition of all the *MPC* curves of firms in a market for a particular good or service will form the market supply curve.

The demand curve for consumers is the marginal private benefit curve (*MPB*). Economists assume that it is possible to measure the benefit obtained from consuming a good by the price people are prepared to pay for it. As an individual consumes more units of a good, the marginal benefit (marginal utility) will fall. This is why the demand curve slopes downwards from left to right. The addition of all the consumers' *MPB* curves for a particular good or service will form the market demand curve.

Market equilibrium occurs where marginal private benefit equals marginal private cost.

The social optimum equilibrium

The social optimum equilibrium level of output or price for a good or service occurs where marginal social cost (*MSC*) equals marginal social benefit (*MSB*). The social cost of producing the last unit of output equals the social benefit from consuming it. When the social optimum is reached in a market, welfare is maximised.

External costs and the triangle of welfare loss

The free market ignores negative externalities. However, adding external costs on to the production of a good or service, such as the production of chemical goods, causes the supply curve of the firm to shift to the left and become the marginal social cost curve, shown in the figure below.

Assuming there are no external benefits in the production of a chemical good, the social optimum price is at OP_1 and quantity OQ_1. When external costs are ignored

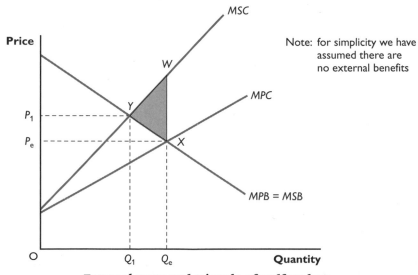

External costs and triangle of welfare loss

there is under-pricing and over-production. There is an excess of social costs over social benefits for the marginal output between Q_e and Q_1.

The marginal social cost of the output slice Q_eQ_1 is Q_eWYQ_1, which exceeds the marginal social benefit of this output Q_eXYQ_1. The excess of social costs over social benefits is shown by the triangle *XWY*. This is the area of welfare loss to society; the market has failed since negative externalities are ignored.

External benefits and the triangle of welfare gain

The free market ignores positive externalities. However, adding external benefits on to the consumption of a good or service, such as the consumption of vaccinations, causes the demand curve to shift to the right and become the marginal social benefit curve, shown in the figure below.

Assuming there are no external costs in the consumption of vaccinations in a free market, the social optimum price is at OP_2 and quantity OQ_2. When external benefits are ignored there is under-pricing and under-production. There is an excess of social benefits over social costs for the marginal output between Q_e and Q_2. Thus, by raising output from OQ_e to OQ_2, welfare could be increased.

The marginal social benefit of the output slice Q_eQ_2 is Q_eMTQ_2, which exceeds the marginal social cost of this output Q_eZTQ_2. The excess of social benefits over social costs is shown by the triangle *MTZ*. This is the area of welfare gain to society; the market has failed since positive externalities are ignored.

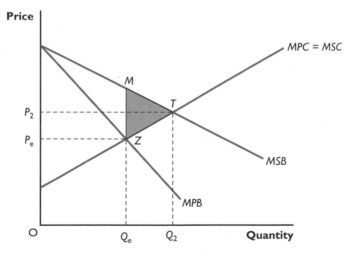

External benefits and triangle of welfare gain

Public goods

Some goods may not be produced at all through the markets, despite offering significant benefits to society. Where this occurs it is known as a 'missing market' and the goods are called **public goods**. These goods involve a large element of collective consumption: for example, national defence, flood defence systems, the criminal justice system and refuse collection.

Public goods are defined by their characteristics of non-excludability and non-rivalry.
- **Non-excludability** means that once a good has been produced for the benefit of one person, it is impossible to stop others from benefiting.
- **Non-rivalry** means that as more people consume a good and enjoy its benefits, it does not reduce the amount available for others. In effect, it is non-diminishable.

Once a public good has been provided, the cost of supplying it to an extra consumer is zero. Further examples are firework displays, lighthouses, public beaches, public parks and street lighting.

Private goods

Private goods are the opposite of public goods. They display characteristics of rivalry and excludability in consumption. An example of a private good is a Mars bar, the consumption of which directly excludes other people from consuming that particular bar. The owners of private goods are able to use private property rights which prevent other people from consuming them. Private goods can also be rejected, which means one has a choice over whether to consume them or not.

The under-provision of public goods

Public goods are under-provided due to two problems.

(1) The free rider problem. Once a public good has been provided for one individual, it is automatically provided for all. The market fails because it is not possible for firms to withhold the good from those consumers who refuse to pay for it. Examples are national defence and security along a street.

The rational consumer would wait for someone else to provide the good and then reap the rewards by consuming it for free. However, if everyone waits for others to supply a public good then it may never be provided. The non-excludability characteristic means that the price mechanism cannot develop as free riders will not pay.

(2) The valuation problem. It is difficult to measure the value obtained by consumers of public goods and hence it becomes hard to establish a market price for them. It is in the interests of consumers to under-value the benefit gained from a public good so that they pay less for it; but it is in the interests of producers to over-value the benefit gained from a public good in order to charge more for it. The uncertainty over valuation may deter firms from providing public goods.

Government provision of public goods

In a mixed economy the government tends to provide public goods in order to correct market failure. It raises funds from general taxation to pay for their provision. Without government intervention, public goods may be under-provided or not provided at all. The actual quantity provided will be less than the amount required for achieving the social optimum position.

Imperfect market knowledge

Symmetric information

In the study of competitive markets it is often assumed that consumers and producers have perfect market information upon which to make their economic decisions. This is known as **symmetric information** — where consumers and producers have perfect and equal market information on a good or service. Assuming that consumers and producers act in a rational way, it will lead to an efficient allocation of resources.

Asymmetric information

In reality, consumers and producers have imperfect and unequal market knowledge upon which to make their economic decisions and this could lead to a misallocation of resources. This is known as **asymmetric information**.

Often producers may know more than consumers about a good or service. A second-hand car salesman, for example, may have greater knowledge of the history of vehicles for sale as well as more technical knowledge than consumers. This could lead to a consumer paying too much for a poor-quality car.

Sometimes consumers may have more market information than producers. For example, a consumer may purchase an insurance policy concealing information about himself or simply know more about his intended future actions. This might include a risky lifestyle.

When there is imperfect market information, markets are likely to fail. This can be seen in the under-consumption of healthcare, education and pensions (sometimes known as **merit goods**) or the over-consumption of tobacco, alcohol and gambling (sometimes known as **demerit goods**).

Labour immobility

The **mobility of labour** refers to the ability of workers to change from one job to another, both geographically and occupationally. There are more than 29 million people working in UK labour markets producing a wide range of goods and services. However, around 1.5 million people are also unemployed, indicating that labour markets do not always operate efficiently.

Some of the unemployed may simply be changing jobs and so register as out of work for a short period of time. After all, the economy is dynamic and specialised, so we should expect some unemployment since jobs are continuously being created and ended. Unemployment while people search for jobs and fill them is known as **frictional unemployment**.

However, a more serious type of unemployment is due to a mismatch of skills and location between job seekers and job providers. This gives rise to immobility of labour and **structural unemployment**.

Geographical immobility refers to the obstacles which prevent labour moving from one area to another to find work. There are several causes, such as family and social ties, the financial costs involved with moving home, imperfect market knowledge on available work, regional variations in house prices and the cost of living. The biggest problem tends to be the lack of affordable housing in many parts of the UK, but especially the southeast region.

Occupational immobility refers to the obstacles which prevent labour from changing their type of occupation to find work. There are several causes, including insufficient education, training, skills and work experience.

Government measures to increase labour mobility

There are various measures that a government might undertake to increase the geographical mobility of labour and these include:

- Relaxation of planning laws which enable construction firms to build housing, especially in green belt areas and the southeast of England.
- Increasing the construction of social housing, such as council properties and charities (housing associations). Rental costs tend to be more affordable than mortgages.
- Offering housing subsidies to certain groups of workers where acute shortages exist, such as teachers, nurses and fire fighters in southeast England. Subsidies may include mortgage relief, shared ownership and relocation grants.
- Improving the operation of Job Centres so that more information is available on job vacancies in any area.

The measures a government might use to increase the occupational mobility of labour include:

- Increasing the provision of training schemes, especially for the unemployed. This might include subsidies to private sector companies to offer training services.
- Increasing the provision of further education, especially in the post-16 sector. Vocational education courses offer training in specific work-based skills and work experience to students.
- Increasing the provision of higher education. There has been a rapid expansion in the number of students in this sector of education over recent years. Increasing access to student loans and limiting tuition fees might help here.

Unstable commodity markets

Commodities refer to raw materials used in the production of goods. They may be minerals and metals such as oil, coal, tin and copper or agricultural goods such as wheat, coffee, tea and sugar. Typically, commodities are used to manufacture goods and services.

Commodity markets are characterised by fluctuating prices and producer incomes which make it difficult to plan future investment programmes and production. This is best shown in agricultural markets where the climate may affect supply in any one year. In the following diagram, initially, planned output is Q_e and price P_e, leading to planned total revenue of OP_eXQ_e.

However, ideal weather increases supply to S_1, causing price to fall to P_1. (Supply is drawn as perfectly price inelastic since the length of the growing season means no more can be produced until the following year.) Total revenue also falls to OP_1YQ_1 since demand for agricultural commodities tends to be price inelastic. Indeed, agricultural goods are often used as ingredients for the production of food — a necessity. A 'good' harvest is a paradox, since farmers are likely to experience a fall in revenue and profits.

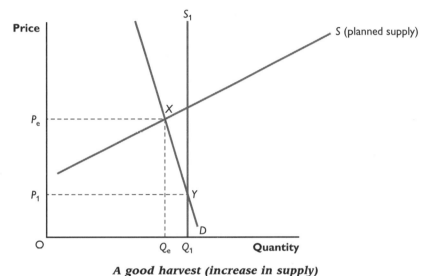

A good harvest (increase in supply)

The next figure shows a poor harvest due to bad weather, which decreases supply to S_2, causing price to rise to P_2. Total revenue also increases to OP_2WQ_2 since demand for agricultural commodities tends to be price inelastic. The 'poor' harvest is a paradox, since farmers are likely to experience a rise in revenue and profits.

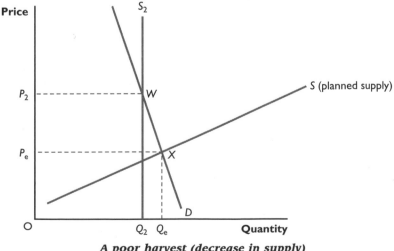

A poor harvest (decrease in supply)

The significance of price and income elasticity of demand

The problem of uncertain supply of commodities in any one year is compounded by the tendency for demand for these type of goods to be price inelastic. As shown previously, a good harvest will lead to a larger fall in price and revenue whereas a poor harvest will lead to a larger rise in price and total revenue. Consequently, farmers may make huge profits one year and huge losses another. It gives rise to market failure.

In the long run, the supply of agricultural commodities has increased dramatically due to major technological innovations: for example, genetically modified crops which increase yield and resistance to drought and pests. However, the growth in demand has failed to keep up with supply. Commodities tend to be income inelastic in demand since each individual has a limited food intake. The implications point to further decreases in the real price of commodities and decreases in revenue for farmers.

However, the rapid economic growth of China and India has helped to increase the demand for commodities and so push up prices and revenues over recent years. The growth in use of biofuels has also led to higher food prices.

The significance of time lags

The length of the growing season for agricultural commodities means there are **time lags** between farmers making the decision to sow seeds or raise livestock and the actual harvest of crops or sale of meat. In a free market this may cause cyclical fluctuations in prices and farm incomes.

Examination skills and concepts

- Defining market failure, external costs and external benefits.
- Distinguishing between private costs and social costs and illustrating them by diagram.
- Distinguishing between private benefits and social benefits and illustrating them by diagram.
- Drawing a diagram to distinguish between the market equilibrium and social optimum equilibrium price and output positions.
- Illustrating the areas of welfare loss and welfare gain on diagrams.
- Applying externalities to different contexts of market failure: for example, transport, healthcare, education, environment, infrastructure projects, waste disposal and recycling.
- Defining public goods, imperfect market information and labour immobility.
- Distinguishing between public goods and private goods.
- Distinguishing between symmetric and asymmetric information.
- Distinguishing between geographical and occupational immobility of labour.
- Drawing diagrams to show price fluctuations in commodity markets.
- Understanding the significance of elasticity in explaining price instability in commodity markets.

Common examination errors

- Incorrect labelling of externality diagrams, confusing external costs and external benefits.
- Identifying the incorrect areas of welfare loss and welfare gain on diagrams.

| Links with other topics |

- Limitations of economic growth as a measure of living standards (Unit 2).
- Costs of economic growth (Unit 2).
- Marginal analysis (Unit 3).
- Price elasticity of demand, income elasticity of demand and price elasticity of supply (Unit 1).

How do governments attempt to correct market failure and what is government failure?

There are various measures a government could undertake to correct market failure: for example, indirect taxation, subsidies, tradable pollution permits, the extension of property rights, regulation, buffer stocks and minimum prices. The relative merits of each measure are now considered in relation to different types of market failure.

Indirect taxation

Indirect taxes are taxes levied on the expenditure of goods or services. The government often imposes taxes on goods which have significant external costs, such as petrol, tobacco and alcohol.

The following diagram shows the market for petrol, including both the marginal private cost curve (MPC) and the marginal social cost curve (MSC). In a free market the equilibrium price is OP_e and the equilibrium quantity OQ_e. However, the social optimum price is OP_1 and the social optimum quantity OQ_1, where marginal social cost (MSC) equals marginal social benefit (MSB) for the last unit produced. The vertical distance ZY represents the external cost (air pollution) for each litre of petrol consumed.

By placing a tax equal to the external cost of ZY per litre, the government successfully internalises the pollution. The total tax collected is shown by the area P_1YZW. Both producers and consumers pay the tax, depending on the relative elasticities of demand and supply. The consumer tax area is YP_1P_eT and the producer tax area is P_eTZW.

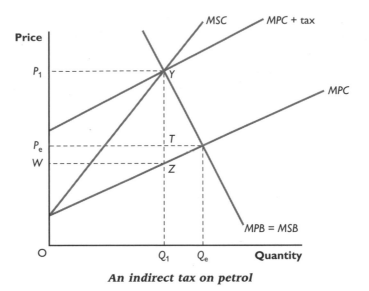

An indirect tax on petrol

Advantages of indirect taxes to correct market failure
- Indirect taxes are based on the principle that the polluters pay — both producer and consumer.
- Indirect taxes work with market forces, helping to internalise the external costs while maintaining consumer choice.
- The level of pollution should fall as output of the good or service is reduced and the price increased — the social optimum position of $MSB = MSC$ can be achieved.
- Tax funds are raised for the government and these can be used to clean up the environment or to compensate the victims of pollution.

Disadvantages of indirect taxes to correct market failure
- It is difficult to quantify the pollution and then place a monetary value on it. Consequently, the social optimum position might not be achieved.
- Indirect taxes increase the costs of production for firms, making them less competitive, compared to firms in other countries where such taxes are not applied.
- Firms may relocate to other countries with less stringent taxes on production.
- The demand for the good or service may be price inelastic and so the overall reduction in pollution levels may be small.
- The tax revenue raised may not be used to compensate victims or clean up the environment.
- It might encourage the development of illegal markets: for example, tobacco and alcohol smuggling to avoid high taxes.

Subsidies

A **subsidy** is a grant provided by the government to encourage the production and consumption of a particular good or service. Subsidies are often applied on goods or services with significant external benefits, such as education and healthcare. They may also be given to alternative forms of economic activity which create less pollution, such as public transport and renewable energy.

Diagram (a) below shows the application of a unit subsidy to the market for electricity from renewable energy sources. The effect of a subsidy is to lower the price of each kilowatt of electricity from P_e to P_1 and increase the quantity from Q_e to Q_1.

The subsidy per unit is AB and the total subsidy area is $ABCP_1$. Part of the subsidy is passed on to consumers in the form of a lower price of electricity, equal to the area AGP_eP_1. The other portion of the subsidy ($GBCP_e$) remains with the producer. The lower price of electricity from renewable energy sources will help decrease the demand for electricity from non-renewable sources from D to D_1 (diagram (b)).

(a) Electricity from renewable energy sources (wind and wave power)

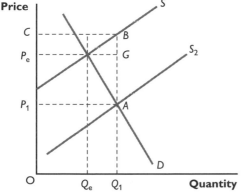

(b) Electricity from non-renewable energy sources (coal and oil)

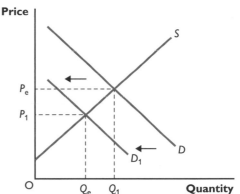

A unit subsidy for renewable electricity generation and the impact on the market for non-renewable electricity generation

Advantages of subsidies applied to renewable energy markets
- They reduce air pollution.
- Using renewable energy sources helps to promote sustained economic growth.
- The rate of consumption of non-renewable resources is reduced.
- Subsidies work with the market. They help to internalise the external benefits from renewable forms of energy.

Disadvantages of subsidies applied to non-renewable energy markets
- There is an opportunity cost to government subsidies. It may lead to higher taxes or cuts in government spending elsewhere.
- Firms may become inefficient in production if they rely upon subsidies.
- Wind power may be a less reliable source of energy than traditional fossil fuels.

Tradable pollution permits (carbon emissions trading)

In 2005 the European Commission set up an **emissions trading system (ETS)** in an attempt to limit greenhouse gas emissions from heavy industry. Its main focus is to curb carbon dioxide emissions by major polluters in the European Union, such as the power generators, steel, paper, cement and ceramics industries. It is intended to include the aviation industry in the scheme in 2012.

The ETS is a 'cap and trade' system. Each year, the European Commission allocates a set amount of carbon dioxidc pcrmits to national governments, which then divide up the allowances among the firms covered by the scheme. This 'caps' the amount of carbon emissions for the year. The pollution permits are **tradable**, which means that firms can buy and sell the allowances between themselves.

Most of the permits have been given free to industry and allocated on the basis of the amount of pollution created before the scheme was created. However, national governments are able to retain up to 10% of carbon permits and offer them for sale depending upon the level of scarcity. The ETS gives an incentive to firms to invest in clean technology and so reduce carbon emissions in the long term.

The ETS also allows firms to invest in schemes that reduce carbon dioxide emissions outside the European Union: for example, in India and China. The savings in carbon emissions can then be offset against their own emissions in the European Union.

Advantages of tradable pollution permits
- A market is created for buying and selling carbon permits, just like other goods and services. In effect, the price mechanism is used to internalise the external costs associated with carbon emissions.
- Pollution permits can be reduced over time as part of a coordinated plan. For example, in 2008 the European Commission cut carbon allocations by 5%.
- National governments can raise funds by selling up to 10% of their pollution permits to industry. The revenue could then be used to clean up the environment or compensate victims.
- Firms have an incentive to invest in clean technology.
- Production costs will increase for firms that exceed their pollution allowances, since they have to purchase additional permits and this provides a source of revenue for cleaner firms that can sell their excess pollution permits.
- The ETS may act as a foundation for a global-wide scheme. It has attracted interest from developed countries outside of the EU. The US state of California intends to join the European scheme.
- Firms may be able to bank their excess pollution permits for use in future years.

Disadvantages of tradable pollution permits
- The European Commission may issue too many carbon permits so that there is little incentive for firms to reduce pollution. This occurred during the first phase of the ETS (2005–07) and led to a collapse in the price of carbon allowances.

- The European Commission may allocate too few carbon permits so that production costs for EU firms increase rapidly, reducing their international competitiveness. Some firms may even relocate outside of the EU to reduce production costs.
- Disputes have arisen over the allocation of carbon permits to firms. Some companies believe they should receive larger allowances and have taken legal proceedings against the European Commission.
- Firms may pass the costs of purchasing pollution permits on to their customers, leading to higher prices of, for example, electricity, steel, glass and paper. This is more likely to happen if demand is price inelastic.
- There is less pressure on major polluting firms to clean up their act if it is possible to buy extra permits from elsewhere.
- EU firms may avoid investing in expensive technology to reduce their own emissions by funding cheaper carbon offsetting schemes in developing countries.
- The price of pollution permits has fluctuated considerably since their inception in 2005. For example, the price of carbon emissions has varied from over €25 to less than €1 per ton. This has created uncertainty among firms about whether to invest heavily in carbon-reducing technology. Firms need a clear guide on what carbon prices will be for the next decade in order to determine their investment levels.
- Pollution permits may create an entry barrier for new firms to enter an industry, so restricting competition.
- There is a cost to the government of monitoring pollution emissions from the many companies within the scheme.
- The European Union is just one part of the world. Unless all countries engage in similar carbon trading schemes, global emissions will continue to increase. In 2007, China became the world's largest carbon polluter; however, it is currently not subject to any limits.
- The valuation of pollution permits is an inexact science. Perhaps it is too important to leave to the market. Much disagreement exists over the costs of greenhouse gas emissions. Some environmental groups believe too little is being done to reduce carbon emissions. Carbon trading is simply leading to a false sense of security.

Carbon offsetting

Carbon offsetting schemes enable consumers or producers to offset their carbon emissions by paying for the removal of the same amount of carbon emissions elsewhere. Many airlines, banks, energy and motor vehicle companies have set up carbon offsetting schemes for their own customers. For example, British Airways customers can pay an additional fee to offset the carbon produced by the flight. This is assumed to be achieved by planting trees, providing solar panels for electricity or replacing light bulbs with energy-efficient versions.

There are several limitations, one being that carbon offsetting is purely voluntary and so customers can ignore the schemes. They are also difficult to regulate and open to widespread fraud. It is also hard to obtain an accurate measure of the emissions to be offset and the effectiveness of the schemes intended to carry this out. Finally, some of the carbon reduction schemes would have occurred irrespective of offsetting.

Renewable energy certificates

Renewable energy obligation certificates (ROCs) were introduced by the government to encourage power-generating firms to use renewable energy sources (e.g. solar, wind, tidal and wave power) to create electricity. Firms are required to have 10% of their power generation from renewable sources by 2010, rising to 15.4% by 2015.

Firms unable to meet the renewable energy target will be obliged to purchase certificates from the government, the proceeds of which are distributed to companies that do meet the target. The purchase price is set at £30 per MWh and will be adjusted in line with the retail price index. This will make renewable energy more price competitive compared to non-renewable energy sources and so promote sustainable economic growth.

Extension of property rights

This involves the government allocating property rights to organisations over the ownership of resources and regarding what uses they can be put to and what rights others have over them. An extension of property rights has been applied to the seas, rivers, mountains and air in certain areas.

All too often negative externalities arise when there is a lack of property rights over a resource. There is an incentive to abuse the use of a resource if there are no property rights: for example, over-fishing in the North Sea.

Advantages of property rights
- Property rights use the market mechanism to ensure an efficient use of resources. This means the owner of the property right will charge consumers and producers for using it.
- There is an increase in the knowledge and expertise for the organisation with the property right. It takes away pressure from the government to assess the pollution.
- There is a greater likelihood that the 'property' (resources) will be managed carefully to ensure its availability for future generations, as with the control of cod catches from the North Sea.
- The property owners can charge firms that need to pollute the environment. The funds can be used to clean up the environment and compensate the sufferers.
- Firms that damage the environment without permission can be prosecuted and made to pay for clean-up operations.

Disadvantages of property rights
- It is often difficult for a government to extend property rights. For example, UK membership of the EU means that EU fishing boats are entitled to fish in UK territorial waters.

- It may be difficult for a government to extend a property right which covers more than one country. For example, the logging of the Amazonian rainforest in Brazil is outside the jurisdiction of developed countries. The external cost which arises cannot easily be internalised.
- It could be difficult to trace the source of environmental damage. In the case of asbestos sufferers who worked for more than one asbestos company, it has been extremely difficult to prove which firm caused the disease. Consequently, compensation payments have been withheld.
- The legal costs involved in prosecuting a polluter could be extremely high, deterring victims from taking action.
- It is difficult to quantify and place a monetary value on the use of a property right and so there could be an incorrect payment made for it. For example, victims of a chemical leak may not get full compensation for the damage caused.

Government regulation

There are various forms of government regulation to correct market failure. In some cases direct controls are applied: for example, the Environmental Protection Act (1989) set minimum environmental standards for emissions from over 3,000 factories involved in chemical processes, waste incineration and oil refining. These firms are monitored by government pollution inspectors who have the power to impose fines and close down factories.

Advantages of regulations
- They are simple to understand: for example, legal restrictions on age limits for the sale of tobacco and alcohol.
- It is possible to fine or close down companies which have abused the regulations: for example, by emitting dangerous levels of toxic waste.
- Consumer protection laws offer some redress against firms that sell shoddy or unsafe goods, or which make false claims about their products. It may help to reduce the problem of asymmetric information.

Disadvantages of regulations
- It is expensive to monitor the behaviour of firms.
- There may be extra costs to firms: for example, the cost of installing pollution monitoring equipment.
- It may be difficult to quantify and attach a monetary value to pollution emissions.
- Regulations prevent the operation of the price mechanism, over-ruling it completely rather than working with it.
- Government failure may occur if the regulations serve to misallocate resources.

Buffer stock schemes

A buffer stock scheme may be operated by a government agency to reduce price fluctuations of a commodity and stabilise producer incomes. It involves the agency setting a target price range for a commodity (a maximum and minimum price) and then intervening to ensure that the price remains within this band despite sudden changes in supply or demand. Examples are coffee, natural rubber, tin and the wool market.

In times of a good harvest (an increase in supply) the price may be in danger of falling too low and so the agency buys up the excess supply of the commodity, adding to its stockpile. In times of a poor harvest (a decrease in supply) the price may be in danger of rising too high and so the agency sells from its stockpile.

Part (a) of the following diagram shows the operation of a buffer stock scheme for cocoa. The initial equilibrium price P_e is within the price range of P_5 and P_3. However, a very good harvest in one year increases supply to Q_1 which causes the price to fall to P_1. The agency intervenes by purchasing quantity XY which prevents the price from falling below the minimum target price P_3. Total agency spending is shown by the area XYQ_1L. It has increased its stockpile of cocoa.

Part (b) shows a poor harvest in another year which decreases supply to Q_6, putting pressure on price to rise to P_6. The agency intervenes by selling quantity VW from its stockpile which prevents price from rising above the maximum target price P_5. Total agency revenue is shown by the area $VWMQ_6$. It has reduced its stockpile of cocoa.

The scheme is meant to be self-financing, since the agency purchases stocks at a low price (P_3) and sells stock at a high price (P_5).

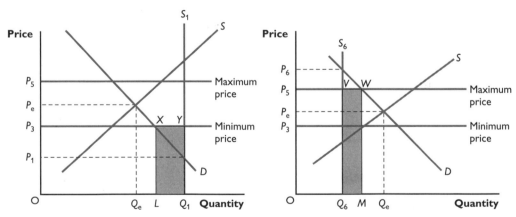

A buffer stock scheme for cocoa

Advantages of buffer stocks
- They reduce commodity price fluctuations, helping to stabilise producer incomes.
- There is greater certainty in the market, leading to more investment.
- They help to ensure provision of commodities for consumers even in years of poor harvests.

Disadvantages of buffer stocks

- A series of good harvests in consecutive years may put too much financial pressure on the agency that has to keep purchasing additional stocks and it may become too expensive to fund. This problem may reflect the initial setting of the price range in the first place — often at too high a level due to asymmetric information between producers and the government agency.
- The long-run trend of increased productivity in the agricultural sector creates a continuous pressure on the agency to purchase additional stocks and requires a downward adjustment of the intervention price range.
- There may be significant costs associated with the storage and security of stockpiles. Usually, large buildings are required.
- The stocks may be perishable over a long period of time, especially agricultural commodities. The agency may lose money by destroying its stocks.
- A series of poor harvests may lead to the agency running out of stocks to release to the market. This means the market price exceeds the maximum price and so the buffer stock system breaks down.

Minimum pricing

The government may stabilise commodity prices and producer incomes through a guaranteed minimum price scheme. For example, EU farmers are guaranteed a minimum price for many commodities, including sugar, wheat and barley. Usually the minimum price is set above the free-market price, causing agricultural surpluses. These are purchased by a government agency at the 'guaranteed' minimum price. This is shown in the diagram.

A minimum price of P_2 causes demand to contract from Q_e to Q_1 and supply to extend from Q_e to Q_2. It leads to an excess supply of Q_1Q_2. Government expenditure on the surplus is shown by the area Q_1Q_2YW and total farm revenue increases from OP_eXQ_e to OP_2YQ_2. The excess supply is stockpiled by the government.

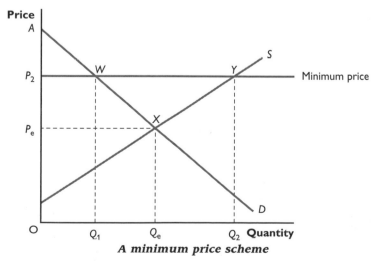

A minimum price scheme

Advantages of a minimum price
- A reduction of commodity price fluctuations makes it easier for consumers to budget their spending.
- Farm incomes are stabilised and increased, leading to greater investment in agriculture.
- Employment in the countryside is maintained, helping to reduce rural–urban inequality.
- Supply of agricultural commodities is guaranteed even in times of poor harvest, due to surplus stockpiles.
- Agricultural surpluses can be used as a form of foreign aid to developing countries.

Disadvantages of a minimum price
- The price of food increases, which could lead to hardship for consumers on low incomes.
- Government spending on agricultural surpluses involves an opportunity cost. It may have to raise taxes or cut spending on other programmes.
- There are increased storage and security costs for the food surpluses.
- The agricultural surpluses may have to be destroyed due to their perishability: for example, milk, fresh peaches and tomatoes.
- The agricultural surpluses may be sold in overseas markets at very low prices. This could damage farmers in developing countries, who are unable to compete against cheap government-owned food.
- Excess supply represents an inefficient allocation of resources.
- Farmers are guaranteed an income which might cause them to become less efficient over time. There is less incentive for farmers to improve the quality of the food or to keep production costs down. All these disadvantages are instances of **government failure**.

Government failure

Government failure occurs if government intervention leads to a net welfare loss. It is where the government causes a misallocation of resources in a market. However, it may be that government failure is less serious than the market failure it tries to cure, as in the case of intervention in tobacco and alcohol markets. Several types of government failure have already been discussed and it is now useful to provide some relevant examples.

High taxation on tobacco, alcohol and waste
High taxes have encouraged illegal smuggling of tobacco and alcohol into the UK. Organised crime has entered these markets, leading to smuggling on a massive scale. The government has lost a significant amount of tax revenue from these illegal activities.

The proposed tax on household waste may sound fine in theory but be unworkable in practice. Some local councils have proposed charging households an extra fee if they have more than two sacks of rubbish collected each week. This could adversely affect large families and low-income households. It could lead to an increase in fly tipping or disputes between households over the ownership of rubbish bags, especially in multi-occupancy properties.

Subsidies to bus transport
Subsidies to bus transport may not lead to a substantial rise in passenger numbers as motorists often prefer the convenience of private car journeys. In some cases, bus transport may be characterised as an inferior good. As real incomes increase, the demand for bus services will fall. This suggests that government subsidies are a waste of taxpayers' money.

Road pricing
A road congestion scheme will help reduce external costs such as traffic congestion and air and noise pollution. However, if the charge is set too high it could lead to an under-utilisation of road space. It may also be unfair to low-income motorists who cannot afford to pay the daily charge. Furthermore, it may reduce trade for businesses within the congestion charge zone. The socially optimum quantity of traffic may not be achieved.

Buffer stocks and minimum prices in agricultural markets
These schemes often lead to huge food surpluses which have to be destroyed or dumped on markets in developing countries. The government has distorted the operation of these markets, leading to an over-supply and misallocation of resources. This also represents a waste of taxpayers' money.

National minimum wage (NMW)
A NMW set above the free-market wage may lead to unemployment in certain labour markets, such as agriculture, textiles, laundry services and security work. The purpose of the NMW is to protect low-paid workers but in some cases it may increase poverty by creating unemployment.

Allocation of fish quotas
The European Commission is responsible for ensuring a sustainable level of fishing in the North Sea by allocating fish catches (quotas) for each commercial fishing boat. However, environmentalists point to depleting fish stocks and blame the government for setting fish quotas at too high a level. There are further problems of fishing boats throwing dead fish back to keep within their quotas and the poor monitoring of fish catches.

Government bureaucracy (red tape)
There are various government rules and regulations, known as 'red tape', that hinder the operation of market forces: for example, concerning proposals for constructing a third runway at Heathrow Airport. Various time-consuming planning enquiries have to be undertaken before major projects can go ahead. This could lead to under-investment in the physical infrastructure of the economy, reducing UK inward investment and UK international competitiveness. It is an example of the time lags involved in making decisions, where the government is too inflexible to respond to the needs of producers and consumers.

Examination skills and concepts

- Understanding different methods of government intervention to correct market failure: for example, indirect taxation, subsidies, tradable pollution permits, property rights, regulation, buffer stocks and minimum pricing.
- Understanding the advantages and disadvantages of government intervention.
- Drawing a diagram to show how a buffer stock scheme operates.
- Drawing a diagram to show how a guaranteed minimum price scheme operates.
- Defining carbon offsetting, renewable energy certificates and government failure.
- Understanding how government failure arises.

Common examination errors

- Incorrect labelling of buffer stock scheme diagrams.
- Imprecise definition of government failure.
- Confusing the consumer and producer tax areas on an indirect tax diagram.

Links with other topics

- Price elasticity of demand, income elasticity of demand and price elasticity of supply (Unit 1).
- Limitations of economic growth as a measure of living standards (Unit 2).
- Conflicts between government economic objectives: for example, economic growth versus sustainability (Unit 2).
- Taxation (Unit 4).

Questions
&
Answers

This section contains four supported multiple-choice question papers and four data-response questions, and is designed to be a key learning, revision and exam preparation resource. You should use these questions to reinforce your understanding of the specification subject matter and as practice for completing work under test conditions.

The multiple-choice questions are similar in structure and style to the Unit 1 examination. However, in the examination each multiple-choice question is placed on a separate page in order to provide room for diagrams and calculations.

A maximum of 4 marks can be scored for each question. Candidates can gain 1 mark for selecting the correct option and 3 marks for explanation. Correct answers are given at the end of the multiple-choice section, together with mark schemes indicating how explanation marks would be awarded.

The data-response questions are also similar in structure and style to the Unit 1 examination. In the exam, you have to answer one from a choice of two data-response questions.

The data-response section includes student answers ranging from grade A to C, and examiner comments explaining, where relevant, how the answer could be improved and a higher grade achieved. These comments are preceded by the icon *e*.

Supported multiple-choice questions

Paper 1 The nature of economics

1 Which of the following is a normative economic statement?

  A Abolishing the 10% income tax rate in April 2008 has reduced the take-home pay of some low-paid workers

  B A change in the rate of income tax affects disposable income

  C Income tax should be increased to 50% for those earning more than £100,000 per year

  D High rates of income tax affect the incentive to work

2

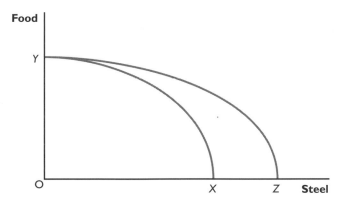

  The diagram shows the production possibility frontier for a country moving from *YX* to *YZ*. The most likely cause of this is:

  A An increase in demand for steel

  B A shift of resources from food to steel production

  C Technological improvements in the steel industry

  D Exhaustion of iron ore deposits used to produce steel

3 Which of the following statements concerning opportunity cost is correct?

  A It is always measured in money terms

  B It occurs in market economies but not mixed economies

  C It indicates that resources are infinite

  D It occurs for both consumers and producers

4 A fast food restaurant carries out labour specialisation in the production of burgers. The purpose of this is to:

  A Achieve benefits from the division of labour

  B Increase the total costs of production

C Achieve benefits from economies of scale

D Increase employment for those who want a job

5 A free-market economy differs from a mixed economy in the following way:

A Business is organised to produce necessities rather than luxuries

B All resources are allocated by the price mechanism

C Essential services such as healthcare and education are provided free to all and funded from taxation

D Most resources are owned and controlled by the government

6 The problem of scarcity could be reduced by:

A Increasing the consumption of energy

B Giving everyone more money

C Government intervention to fix the price of goods

D The discovery of more resources

7 Which of the following is a positive economic statement?

A There is an opportunity cost to increasing government spending on defence

B Increasing university tuition fees is fair

C The provision of public goods should be left to market forces

D A private healthcare system works better than the National Health Service

8

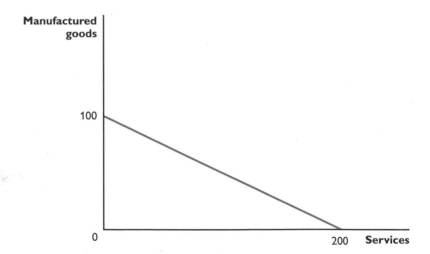

The diagram above shows a production possibility frontier for a country. Which of the following statements is true?

A The output of manufactured goods will equal the output of services

B The opportunity cost of one extra unit of manufactured good increases as output increases

C There is a constant rate of consumer demand for both manufactured goods and services

D There is a constant rate of opportunity cost between manufactured goods and services

Paper 2 The demand for goods and services

1 Which of the following will cause an increase in the price of steel without shifting its supply curve?   TIS C

- **A** An increase in indirect tax on steel
- **B** An increase in the price of iron ore, the raw material used to produce steel
- **C** The withdrawal of a subsidy for steel producers
- **D** An increase in the price of steel substitutes, such as aluminium and tin

2

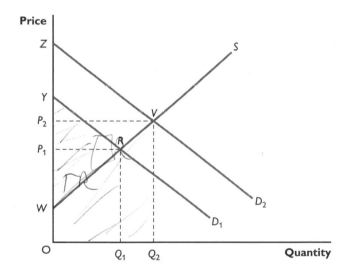

The diagram above shows the market for wheat. A shift in the demand curve for wheat from D_1 to D_2 will cause:

- **A** An increase in total revenue
- **B** A decrease in producer surplus
- **C** A decrease in demand for wheat ✕
- **D** A decrease in consumer surplus

3 The owner of a cinema decides to reduce the price of each ticket from £6 to £3. This causes ticket sales to increase for each showing from 200 to 400.

The best estimate for price elasticity of demand is:

- **A** −0.5
- **B** −1.0
- **C** −1.5
- **D** −2.0

$$\frac{200}{50\%}$$

S upported multiple-choice paper 2

4 The table shows the income elasticities of demand for selected UK holiday destinations.

Holiday destination	Income elasticity of demand	
Bournemouth	2.0	Normal
Newquay	0.6	
Margate	−0.4	Inferior

It may be deduced from the data in the table that:
A All the holiday destinations are normal goods ✗
B Holidays in Bournemouth are price elastic in demand ✗
Ⓒ A decrease in real income will cause a decrease in demand for holidays in Newquay
D There is a negative cross elasticity of demand for holidays in Margate

5 If the price elasticity of demand for coffee is −0.4 and the cross elasticity of demand between tea and coffee is +0.5, a 10% decrease in the price of coffee will cause:
A A 4% fall in demand for coffee and the demand for tea to rise by 5%
Ⓑ A 4% rise in demand for coffee and the demand for tea to fall by 5%
C A 40% rise in demand for coffee and the demand for tea to fall by 50%
D A 0.4% fall in demand for coffee and the demand for tea to rise by 0.5%

−0.4
+0.5 —

6 The following table shows the demand and supply schedules for a good. (You may use the blank column in your explanation).

Price per unit (£)	Quantity demanded (units)	Quantity supplied (units)	New quantity demanded (units)
10	200	1,800	600
9	400	1,600	800
8	600	1,400	1,000
7	800	1,200	1,200
6	1,000	1,000	1,400
5	1,200	800	1,600
4	1,400	600	1,800

An increase in demand of 400 units at every price level will cause:
A An increase in the equilibrium price but not quantity
Ⓑ An increase in the equilibrium quantity but not price
C An increase in the equilibrium price and quantity
D Equilibrium price and quantity to remain constant

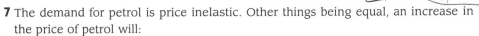

7 The demand for petrol is price inelastic. Other things being equal, an increase in the price of petrol will:

  A Decrease total consumer spending on petrol

  B Increase demand for motor vehicles

  C Increase total revenue for petrol companies

  D Decrease costs of production for road haulage companies

8 Assuming there are normal demand and supply curves for a good, an increase in consumer demand is likely to:

  A Decrease consumer surplus

  B Discourage new firms from entering the market

  C Decrease market price

  D Increase producer surplus

Paper 3 The supply of goods and services

1 Which of the following will cause the price of strawberries to fall without a shift in the demand curve?

  A An increase in the price of fresh cream, a complement to strawberries

  B An decrease in the productivity of strawberry farm workers

  C An increase in the price of cherries, a substitute for strawberries

  D A decrease in the wages of strawberry farm workers

2

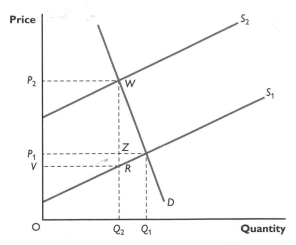

The diagram shows a tax placed on tobacco which shifts the supply curve from S_1 to S_2. Which of the following is correct about the nature and incidence of the tax?

  A It is *ad valorem*, the incidence falling mainly on tobacco producers

  B It is specific, the incidence falling mainly on tobacco consumers

  C It is *ad valorem*, the incidence falling mainly on tobacco consumers

  D It is specific, the incidence falling mainly on tobacco producers

3 Good X has a very low price elasticity of supply. Which of the following is most likely to be good X?

A A newspaper, because it forms a relatively insignificant part of the total expenditure of a household

B Toothpaste, because it has no close substitutes

C Fresh tomatoes, since they are a perishable agricultural good

D Alcohol, because it is an addictive good

4

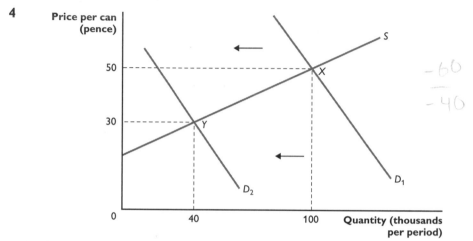

The diagram shows the demand and supply curves for a local fizzy drinks firm. The equilibrium position is initially X but following a decrease in demand from D_1 to D_2 and a fall in market price, the firm intends to reduce production to point Y. The best estimate for price elasticity of supply is:

A 1.5

B −0.66

C −1.5

D 0.66

5

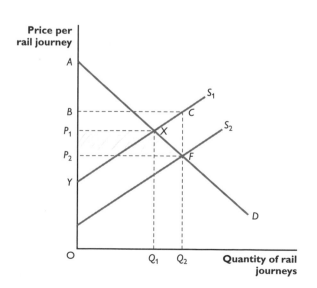

The diagram shows a unit subsidy placed on rail travel between London and Bath, shifting the supply curve from S_1 to S_2. Which of the following is correct?

A Consumer surplus increases by P_1P_2FX

B The total subsidy area is OP_2FQ_2

C Producer surplus increases to P_1XY

D The rail fare falls by the same amount as the unit subsidy

6 Which of the following will cause the price of diamonds to rise without shifting the demand curve?

A Discovery of new diamond resources in South Africa

B A decrease in the price of platinum jewellery

C The diamond company De Beers reducing its stockpile of diamonds

D An increase in mining costs for extracting diamonds

7

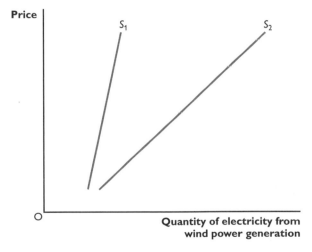

The diagram shows how the price elasticity of supply of electricity from wind power generation may vary over time. Which of the following is most likely to be true?

A Price elasticity of supply is unitary along each supply curve

B S_1 is likely to be the short-run supply curve and S_2 the long-run supply curve

C Price elasticity of supply remains constant along each supply curve

D S_1 is perfectly price inelastic in supply and S_2 perfectly price elastic in supply

8 The table shows the demand and supply schedules for a luxury range of caviar. (You may use the blank column for your explanation).

Price per unit (£)	Quantity demanded (boxes)	Quantity supplied (boxes)	New quantity supplied (boxes)
50	120	240	
40	140	220	
30	160	200	
20	180	180	
10	200	160	

If the government introduces an indirect tax of £20 per box of caviar, the tax revenue obtained will be:

A £4,400
B £3,600
C £3,200
D £2,800

Paper 4 Market failure and government failure

1 All of the following are examples of market failure *except*:
A External costs and benefits
B Under-provision of public goods
C Geographical and occupational immobility of labour
D Unemployment created by the national minimum wage

2 A flood defence scheme for London is *unlikely* to be provided in a free-market economy. This may be because of:
A A shortage of drinking water
B The free rider problem
C The ability to charge households for their individual consumption
D A lack of technology for constructing the flood barrier

3 The table shows the demand and supply schedules for barley, an agricultural good.

Price (£)	Quantity demanded (million tons)	Quantity supplied (million tons)
140	20	24
120	21	23
100	22	22
80	23	21
60	24	20

A government agency introduces a guaranteed minimum price at £120 per ton, leading to:
A An increase in government agency spending
B A decrease in price
C An excess demand
D A decrease In supply

4 A negative externality exists when:
A The consumption of a product provides benefits to third parties
B The social cost exceeds the private cost in production
C Costs are internalised by the price mechanism
D The social cost is less than the private cost in consumption

5

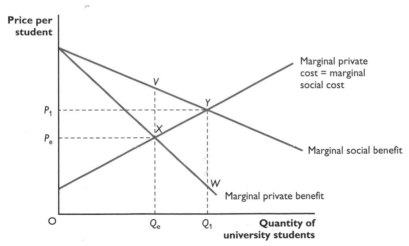

The diagram shows the market for university education. Assume there are no external costs and no government intervention. Which of the following is correct?
A There is an over-consumption of university education
B Private benefits exceed social benefits
C Welfare can be increased by raising the quantity of students from Q_e to Q_1
D External benefits exceed social benefits

6

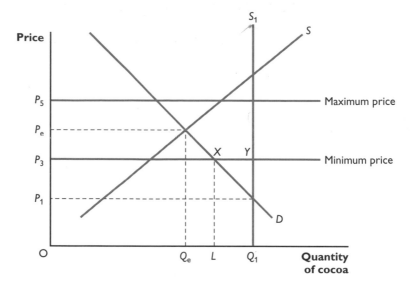

The diagram shows the operation of a buffer stock scheme for cocoa by an agency. Following a good harvest, supply increases to S_1 for a given year. The agency will:
A Allow the market price of cocoa to increase to P_5
B Reduce its stockpile of cocoa
C Allow the market price of cocoa to decrease to P_1
D Add to its stockpile of cocoa

7 Tradable pollution permits may be ineffective in reducing carbon dioxide emissions within the European Union if:
A Firms find it difficult to relocate production outside of the EU
B There is an excess demand for pollution permits
C It is easy to monitor carbon emissions from firms
D Supply exceeds demand for pollution permits

8 There may be under-consumption of fruit and vegetables in a free market due to:
A Symmetrical information between producers and consumers
B A government subsidy to fruit and vegetable producers
C Imperfect market information
D The market output exceeding the social optimum output

Answers to multiple-choice papers

Up to 2 explanation marks can be gained by knocking out 2 incorrect options.

Paper 1

Question 1
Correct answer C. (1 mark)

Definition of normative statement. **(1 mark)**

Includes the term 'should' and so is normative. **(1 mark)**

The others are positive statements and so are based on asserting facts. **(1 mark)**

Question 2
Correct answer C. (1 mark)

Definition of production possibility frontier. **(1 mark)**

The potential output of steel has increased. **(1 mark)**

New technology could lead to more efficient machinery and plant. **(1 mark)**

Question 3
Correct answer D. (1 mark)

Definition of opportunity cost. **(1 mark)**

Application to consumer (for example, £10 spent on burger meal means forgoing spending £10 on a new scarf). **(1 mark)**

Application to producer (for example, investing £1m on new machinery means £1m less funds for shareholder dividends). **(1 mark)**

Question 4
Correct answer A. (1 mark)

Definition of division of labour. **(1 mark)**

Application and explanation of two benefits of division of labour for burger restaurant (for example, shorter training period per task, more efficient use of tills and deep fat fryers or that repetition increases expertise and so raises productivity). **(1 + 1 marks)**

Question 5
Correct answer B. (1 mark)

Definition of free-market economy other than that offered in correct option (for example, demand and supply determines resource allocation with no government intervention). **(1 mark)**

Application (for example, the price mechanism would provide all education and healthcare services). **(1 mark)**

Identify a mixed economy as one with both a public and private sector. **(1 mark)**

Question 6
Correct answer D. (1 mark)

Definition of scarcity. **(1 mark)**

Application and explanation of discovery of new resources (for example, vast new

deposits of oil and gas discovered in the Falklands could help alleviate shortage of energy for production of goods and services). **(1 + 1 marks)**

Question 7

Correct answer A. (1 mark)

Definition of positive statement. **(1 mark)**

Application to opportunity cost (for example, increased defence spending might mean less funds available for education). **(1 mark)**

The others are normative statements and so are based on value judgements. **(1 mark)**

Question 8

Correct answer D. (1 mark)

Definition of production possibility frontier or opportunity cost. **(1 mark)**

Application and explanation of constant opportunity cost, since gradient is constant. **(1 mark)**

One manufactured good costs the output of two services. **(1 mark)**

Paper 2

Question 1

Correct answer D. (1 mark)

An increase in the price of tin and aluminium will cause an increase in demand for substitutes such as steel. **(1 mark)**

Other things being equal, an increase in demand for steel will push up the price. **(1 mark)**

Application with demand and supply diagram. **(1 mark)**

Also accept positive cross elasticity of demand discussion. **(1 mark)**

Question 2

Correct answer A. (1 mark)

Definition of total revenue. **(1 mark)**

Original total revenue OP_1RQ_1. **(1 mark)**

New total revenue OP_2VQ_2. **(1 mark)**

Question 3

Correct answer D. (1 mark)

Definition or formula of PED. **(1 mark)**

Workings of calculation ($+100\% \div -50\% = -2$). **(1+1 marks)**

Question 4

Correct answer C. (1 mark)

Definition or formula of YED. **(1 mark)**

Holidays to Newquay are a normal good with a positive YED. **(1 mark)**

Application (for example, a 10% fall in income causes a 6% fall in demand for holidays in Newquay). **(1 mark)**

Also accept holidays to Newquay are income inelastic in demand since it is less than 1. **(1 mark)**

Question 5
Correct answer B. (1 mark)

Definition or formula for PED or XED. **(1 mark)**

Workings of calculations (for example, +4% ÷ −10% = −0.4 for coffee). **(1 mark)**

Calculation of −5% ÷ −10% = 0.5 for tea. **(1 mark)**

Also accept that tea and coffee are substitutes with a positive XED. **(1 mark)**

Question 6
Correct answer C. (1 mark)

Original equilibrium price is £6 and quantity 1,000. **(1 mark)**

New equilibrium price rises to £7 and quantity to 1,200. **(1+1 marks)**

This may be shown by completion of blank column provided.

Question 7
Correct answer C. (1 mark)

Definition or formula of PED. **(1 mark)**

Explanation of rise in total revenue (for example, percentage rise in price is greater than percentage fall in demand). **(1 mark)**

Diagram showing an increase in total revenue. **(1 mark)**

Question 8
Correct answer D. (1 mark)

Definition of producer surplus. **(1 mark)**

Application and explanation by diagram showing an increase in demand with original and new levels of producer surplus. **(1+1 marks)**.

Paper 3

Question 1
Correct answer D. (1 mark)

A decrease in wages will lower the unit cost of strawberries. **(1 mark)**

This increases the supply curve. **(1 mark)**

The result is a reduction of the price. **(1 mark)**

Also marks available for a diagram showing an increase in supply and a decrease in price. **(1 + 1 marks)**

Question 2
Correct answer B. (1 mark)

Definition of specific tax. **(1 mark)**

Consumers pay tax area P_1P_2WZ. **(1 mark)**

Producers pay tax area P_1ZRV. **(1 mark)**

A mark for the idea of specific tax since it is a parallel shift in supply curve. **(1 mark)**

Producers pay most of the tax since demand is price elastic. **(1 mark)**

Question 3
Correct answer C. (1 mark)

Definition or formula of PES. **(1 mark)**

Explanation and application of low PES for fresh tomatoes (for example, cannot be stored, so no spare stocks and long time period needed to grow). **(1 + 1 marks)**

Explanation of low PES in terms of inelastic supply. **(1 mark)**

Question 4

Correct answer A. (1 mark)

Definition or formula of PES. **(1 mark)**

Workings of calculation ($-60\% \div -40\% = 1.5$). **(1 + 1 marks)**

Explanation that supply is price elastic. **(1 mark)**

Question 5

Correct answer A. (1 mark)

Definition of consumer surplus. **(1 mark)**

Original consumer surplus is AXP_1. **(1 mark)**

The new level of consumer surplus is AFP_2. **(1 mark)**

Question 6

Correct answer D. (1 mark)

Increase in mining costs means higher production costs. **(1 mark)**

Supply shifts vertically upwards. **(1 mark)**

This causes an increase in price. **(1 mark)**

A diagram showing a decrease in supply and an increase in price. **(1 + 1 marks)**

Question 7

Correct answer B. (1 mark)

Definition or formula of PES. **(1 mark)**

S_1 is short-run supply where at least one factor input is fixed, so supply cannot easily respond to a rising price. **(1 mark)**

S_2 is long-run supply where all factor inputs are variable, so supply can respond more easily to a rise in price. **(1 mark)**

Application to wind power (takes time to gain planning permission and construct more wind turbines). **(1 mark)**

Question 8

Correct answer C. (1 mark)

Definition of indirect tax. **(1 mark)**

Workings of calculation ($160 \times £20 = £3,200$). **(1+1 marks)**

Identifying the new equilibrium price of £30. **(1 mark)**

Paper 4

Question 1

Correct answer D. (1 mark)

Definition of government failure. **(1 mark)**

Explanation of NMW leading to a contraction in demand and extension in supply of labour, creating unemployment. **(1 + 1 marks)**

Diagrammatic analysis. **(1 + 1 marks)**

Question 2
Correct answer B. (1 mark)

Definition of a public good. **(1 mark)**
Explanation and application of the free-rider problem to a flood defence scheme. **(1 + 1 marks)**

Question 3
Correct answer A. (1 mark)

Definition of a guaranteed minimum price. **(1 mark)**
Excess supply is created which government has to purchase to ensure scheme remains in operation. **(1 mark)**
Calculation of government spending on the scheme (£120 × 2 million tons = £240 million). **(2 marks)**

Question 4
Correct answer B. (1 mark)

Definition of a negative externality. **(1 mark)** A relevant diagram. **(1 mark)**
Explanation that social costs include both private and external costs. **(1 mark)**
Application to an example of an external cost (such as pollution). **(1 mark)**

Question 5
Correct answer C. (1 mark)

Definition of welfare gain (social benefit exceeds social cost). **(1 mark)**
Application and explanation to increase quantity by Q_eQ_1 (for example, social benefit Q_eQ_1YV exceeds social cost Q_eQ_1YX). **(1 + 1 marks)**

Question 6
Correct answer D. (1 mark)

Definition of buffer stocks scheme. **(1 mark)**
Agency will purchase XY or LQ_1 of cocoa at the minimum price P_3. **(1 + 1 marks)**
The total area of agency spending is equal to XYQ_1L. **(1 mark)**

Question 7
Correct answer D. (1 mark)

Definition of tradable pollution permit. **(1 mark)**
If supply exceeds demand, there is a downward pressure on the price of tradable permits. **(1 mark)**
There is less incentive for firms to cut back on pollution. **(1 mark)**
Total supply could exceed demand, causing price to fall to zero. **(1 mark)**

Question 8
Correct answer C. (1 mark)

Imperfect market information is a market failure leading to an inefficient allocation of resources. **(1 mark)**
Explanation of imperfect market information. **(1 mark)**
Consumers may have fewer fruit and vegetables than is required for a healthy diet. **(1 mark)**

Data-response questions

Question 1   The housing market in England

Table 1 Average house price, annual earnings and employment level by region, April 2008

Region	Average property price	Average earnings[a]	Number in employment (thousands)[b]
North	£159,116	£20,951	1,170
Yorks & Humber	£169,974	£21,960	2,460
North West	£176,432	£22,579	3,203
East Midlands	£180,387	£21,851	2,144
West Midlands	£199,605	£22,360	2,507
East Anglia	£232,599	£23,400	2,829
South West	£261,919	£22,246	2,579
South East	£303,749	£24,997	4,194
Greater London	£403,545	£30,207	3,712
England	£239,581	£23,749	24,798

Sources: www.Rightmove.co.uk and www.ONS.org.uk

[a] Figures on annual earnings are for 2007.

[b] Figures on employment levels are for January 2008, Labour Force Survey.

Extract 1 Falling house prices

House prices fell by 2.5% in March 2008, the fifth consecutive month. They could fall by a further 25% over the next 2 years, particularly if the banks continue to tighten up on the availability of mortgage loans (house loans) and consumer confidence drops further. Unemployment is also expected to increase from 5.3% to 7.5% of the workforce over the next 2 years, further depressing the housing market.

In such an economic climate, most building firms have cut back on new housing projects and reduced their staff. It has also affected the retail sector. IKEA, the Swedish home furnishing firm, has delayed opening up new stores. It is now concentrating on expansion in central Europe. Many people intending to sell their properties have taken them off the market.

> ### Extract 2 Regional inequality
>
> Regional house price differences remain. This has led to shortages of skilled workers in Greater London, especially in the nursing, teaching and firefighter professions.
>
> Many first-time buyers cannot afford property in Greater London and so are forced to rent or live elsewhere. Often these are young and dynamic workers, essential for wealth creation. In many cases, people can borrow up to three times their annual income for a mortgage; but this is nowhere near enough for first-time buyers, who tend to be in the early stages of their careers.
>
> However, the enlargement of the European Union in 2004 has led to a significant net migration inflow to the UK from central and eastern Europe. This has helped to reduce labour shortages.

(a) With reference to Extract 1, explain why house prices in England are expected to fall over the next 2 years. Use a demand and supply diagram in your answer. **(6 marks)**

(b) Examine the likely economic effects of falling house prices on:
   (i) the market for building workers **(5 marks)**
   (ii) the market for home furnishings **(5 marks)**

(c) With reference to Extract 2 and Table 1, select two regions and examine two possible reasons why average house prices differ between them. **(12 marks)**

(d) To what extent might regional house price differences cause market failure? **(10 marks)**

(e) Discuss the possible economic effects of falling house prices on:
   (i) first-time buyers **(5 marks)**
   (ii) the private rental market **(5 marks)**

■ ■ ■

Candidate's answer

(a) House prices are likely to fall due to a decrease in demand. The diagram shows a decrease in demand for housing from D to D_1, causing prices to fall from P_e to P_1. This is a result of the credit crunch where banks have been hit by people not repaying their loans. The banks have made it much harder for people to obtain a mortgage and so there is falling demand for housing. Also, there is very low consumer confidence and expectations of rising unemployment. In such an environment people are unlikely to buy houses. **6/6 marks**

d ata-response question 1

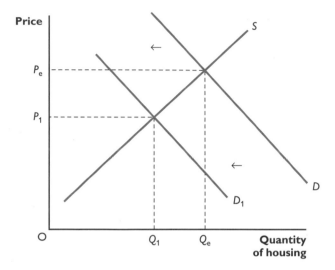

Price — vertical axis; Quantity of housing — horizontal axis; curves S, D, D_1; levels P_e, P_1; quantities Q_1, Q_e; origin O.

✍ A sound answer. The candidate draws and labels the diagram accurately and uses information from the extract to explain the reasons for the fall in house prices (harder to borrow, falling consumer confidence, rising unemployment). This candidate would receive 3 marks for the diagram and its explanation, and 3 marks for reasons why demand falls.

(b) (i) The market for building workers is likely to decline. The decrease in demand for houses will cause a decrease in demand for building workers. This is because labour is a derived demand. It is not wanted for its own sake but rather for what it produces. The fall in demand for houses has led to a reduction in house prices. Building firms may also reduce wages to cut their costs of production and restore some of their profits. The extent of the decrease in demand for building workers depends on the magnitude of the decrease in demand for houses and the fall in price. It seems that a big price fall of 25% is expected over the next 2 years, so a lot of building workers are going to lose their jobs. **5/5 marks**

✍ A good answer. The candidate uses the concept of 'derived demand' and adds value to the general view of a fall in demand and wages for building workers. An evaluative comment is also offered by considering the magnitude of the decline. (3 marks for the impact on the labour market; 2 marks for evaluation.)

(ii) The market for home furnishings is also likely to decline. This is shown by IKEA cutting back on its investment plans to open new stores. It has already experienced a fall in demand for furniture and so there is little point expanding in England. There are less people buying furniture for their new homes. This means IKEA receives less revenue and profits and so might even cut back on production. It might also cut its prices. This is one of the functions of the price mechanism, namely, to indicate changes in demand to producers, who respond by reallocating their resources.

In evaluation, the impact on the home furnishings market depends upon how much of it is based on people moving into new homes. A lot of people buy furniture without moving home so the overall impact might be small. However, IKEA has announced plans to stop building new stores in England so there must be some effect. Also, IKEA might be looking at the long term and realise that house prices are set to fall for at least 2 years.   **5/5 marks**

📝 A sound answer. The candidate adds value to the answer by considering the effect on profits, prices and output in home furnishings. The second paragraph is mainly evaluation. The candidate helps the examiner to recognise this by stating that it is an evaluative comment. (3 marks for explanation; 2 marks for evaluation.)

(c) Large differences in regional house prices exist in England. Average house prices in Greater London (£403,545) are 2.5 times more expensive than for the North (£159,116). This is a really big difference and probably reflects the differences in regional income and wealth. On average people earn a higher income in Greater London (£30,207) than the North (£20,951) and so can afford to take out bigger mortgages and pay more for houses. The ratio of average earnings between Greater London and the North is 1.44 to 1. Also there is a lot of wealth built up in houses over many years in Greater London. When people move homes in Greater London they probably have a lot of wealth in the house to take with them to put as a deposit on their new home.

A second reason might be due to the greater scarcity of land for building on in Greater London compared to the North. There are very tight planning restrictions in Greater London since it is already a big urban area and so not much land becomes available to build on. This means demand will tend to exceed supply, pushing up the price of land. In the North there is more land available to build on so the price of this is lower, reducing the costs of building houses. This will lead to lower house prices.

The higher level of demand compared to supply between the two regions is shown in the diagram. The house price equilibrium is much higher in Greater London.

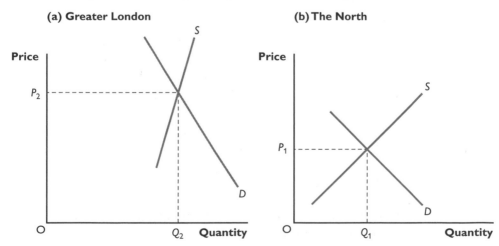

(a) Greater London   **(b) The North**

79

Both of the reasons given are very important causes of regional house price differences. I think differences in income and wealth are the most significant since it will determine how much people can borrow and spend on buying a house. One could note that there are other possible factors that help explain regional house price differences such as employment levels, investment levels and the costs of living. **12/12 marks**

🖉 A sound answer. The candidate uses Table 1 to calculate the regional house price ratio between Greater London and the North. Then he/she investigates two possible causes of regional house price differences and offers diagrammatic analysis. Table 1 is used again to discuss the relevance of regional earnings data. Finally, some evaluation is offered by prioritising between the two causes and opening up the possibility of further determinants of regional differences. The candidate could have discussed the significance of regional employment levels as shown in Table 1 but decided not to. This candidate would receive 4 + 4 marks for use of data and analysis of the two reasons; and 2 + 2 marks for evaluation.

(d) Market failure is when the price mechanism fails to allocate resources efficiently. The market mechanism leads to a misallocation of resources. Regional house price differences on such a large scale cause a market failure. This is because it leads to a geographical immobility of labour — where labour from the northern regions cannot afford to move to Greater London and take up work since they cannot pay for housing. Staff shortages exist in fire fighting, nursing and teaching in Greater London, which reduce the quality of services provided. In the long term, it could seriously reduce the quality of human capital, leading to lower productivity and competitiveness. Firms might find they cannot fill job vacancies and cut back on expansion plans or even leave the region. To make a more effective evaluation it is necessary to have further information on the number of staff shortages in different occupations in Greater London. Also, labour shortages could well exist in all regions of England, not just Greater London.

Extract 2 refers to the large scale immigration into the UK following the expansion of the European Union in 2004. This has helped reduce the shortage of labour in Greater London and elsewhere. Also, it indicates that the problem of regional house price differences can be partly overcome through market forces of labour migration to the UK. **10/10 marks**

🖉 A sound answer. The candidate starts by defining market failure and then explains the problem of geographical immobility of labour before discussing how high house prices in Greater London have created shortages of key workers. The problems of labour immobility help justify it as a form of market failure. Evaluation marks are gained for explaining what further information is needed to come to a decision. The candidate also evaluates by suggesting that labour immigration has helped reduce the staff shortages. This is the market mechanism in action. This candidate would receive 2 marks for market failure definition, 4 marks for analysis and a further 2 + 2 marks for evaluation points.

(e) (i) A decrease in house prices should be good news for first-time buyers since it means housing becomes more affordable. Property buyers are usually limited to borrowing up to three times their annual income and so it depends on whether house prices will fall enough and whether their income is high enough to get on the property ladder. Extract 1 suggests that house prices could fall by 25% over the next 2 years. Hopefully, this will be enough for first-time buyers.

However, Extract 2 points out that many first-time buyers are at an early stage of their career and so presumably they have not reached their maximum earnings potential. This could make it really hard to buy a property. On the other hand, the house-price data shown in Table 1 is only an average. There must be cheaper properties in each region, for example, 1 bedroom flats and apartments or properties in run down areas. Perhaps first-time buyers need to consider these properties to get on the housing ladder. **5/5 marks**

A sound answer. The candidate refers to the information provided to develop an argument. He/she considers the pros and cons of falling house prices for first-time buyers. Considering both views is a form of evaluation. This candidate would receive 3 marks for explanation and 2 marks for evaluation.

(ii) A decrease in house prices might cause the private rental market to decline. This is because buying and renting properties are substitutes for each other with a positive cross elasticity of demand. A decrease in demand for rental property may force landlords to reduce their rents and some will decide it is not worth staying in the market. Supply of rented accommodation might contract.

However, it depends on how close privately owned and rental property are as substitutes for each other. Even a 25% fall in property prices will not be enough for many people to afford to buy. This is especially the case since banks are now very reluctant to lend out new mortgages. Also, a lot of people may not really want to risk buying at a time of rising unemployment and low consumer confidence. Furthermore, the fall in property prices is forecast over 2 years. This will give plenty of time for landlords to meet the new competition by improving their own accommodation. Also, property prices are difficult to predict and the forecast could be wrong.

Finally, some people prefer to rent property since it makes them more geographically mobile in terms of changing jobs. **5/5 marks**

A sound answer. The candidate recognises that privately owned and rental properties are substitutes and explores possible consequences, using economic analysis. There are lots of evaluation points too: for example, discussing the size of the predicted property price fall and whether it will really happen or whether it matters since banks have cut back on house loans. One feature of a good answer is the element of caution offered throughout. The candidate tends to refer to events that 'may' occur rather than 'will' occur. This is a useful point to remember when answering data-related questions. This candidate would receive 3 explanation marks and 2 evaluation marks.

Total score: 48/48 = grade A

Question 2   The oil and petrol markets

Figure 1 The price of a litre of petrol (107.9 pence)

Price of a litre of petrol (pence)

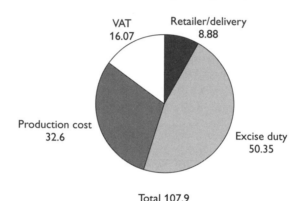

Total 107.9

Source: www.petrolprices.com 2007

Extract 1 Soaring oil prices

The days of cheap oil are over. Oil prices have almost risen fivefold over the past 4 years from $25 a barrel in 2004 to over $122 in the summer of 2008. Barely a decade ago, oil was just $10 a barrel. The soaring oil price is due to a combination of demand and supply conditions. Industrialisation of China and India has led to growing consumption. Indeed, China is now the world's third largest consumer of oil, sucking in 7.5 million barrels a day. Instability in the Middle East — a major oil-producing region — has also led to speculative buying and disruption to supplies. A major pipeline exporting oil from Basra in Iraq was recently blown up by terrorists. Many existing oil fields are also running dry: for example, production in the North Sea is now declining.

At $122 a barrel, oil is directing huge sums of money from consumers to producers, mainly in the Middle East. Oil exports from this region are now worth $750 billion a year. The Saudi Arabian government is building four new cities and improving its infrastructure. The oil-producing countries have so much cash that they are buying

Western assets. These investments are estimated at $2,000 billion and could rise to $12,000 billion by 2012 according to the International Monetary Fund.

Chakib Khelil, president of OPEC (Organisation of Petroleum Exporting Countries), a producer cartel, has warned that prices could reach $200 a barrel over the next year. The cartel has refused to raise production, increasing the possibility of a global recession.

Extract 2 Rising petrol prices

Rising oil prices have caused a knock-on effect in other markets. The price of petrol (which is made from refining oil) has risen by more than 25% over the past 4 years in the UK, to £1.08 per litre. Government ministers are preparing for fuel protests by motorists, similar to those in the year 2000. This disrupted fuel supplies to petrol stations so that people could not get to work.

Gas and electricity prices have also risen sharply: Npower, one of Britain's major energy suppliers, raised gas and electricity bills to households by 17.2% and 12.7% respectively in 2008. Food prices are up by 5.3% on a year ago, since rising energy prices add to the cost of food production and distribution.

However, technology may come to the rescue in the long term as alternative sources of energy are developed. The government is providing more than £500 million in subsidies to the construction of wind and wave power farms over the next few years. Motor vehicles are also becoming more fuel efficient and there has been a rush to develop biofuels. These use cereals to produce oil for motor vehicles. Electric-powered cars are also becoming more fashionable in urban areas. This may help reduce the dependency on oil.

(a) (i) **Using a supply and demand diagram, explain why 'oil prices have almost risen fivefold over the past 4 years' (Extract 1, lines 1–2).** (8 marks)

  (ii) **Examine the effects of soaring oil prices on the producers of oil.** (6 marks)

(b) **Using the information provided, assess two possible reasons why petrol prices have risen at a slower rate than oil prices.** (6 marks)

(c) **Examine the likely economic effects of an increase in indirect taxation on the market for petrol. Use a supply and demand diagram in your answer.** (10 marks)

(d) **To what extent is the tax on petrol an example of government failure?** (10 marks)

(e) **With reference to Extract 2, discuss how the price elasticity of demand for oil might change over time.** (8 marks)

■ ■ ■

Candidate's answer

(a) (i) The price of oil has soared over the past 4 years due to changes in conditions of demand and supply. There have been significant increases in demand for oil as China and India industrialise and so need more fuel to keep growing. Uncertainty over supply from the Middle East has also led to speculative demand for oil. These factors have caused the demand curve to increase from D_1 to D_2. The supply of oil has also decreased due to the exhaustion of major oil fields, for example, the North Sea and terrorist attacks in the Middle East. OPEC, a producer cartel, has refused to raise production, so putting more pressure on oil prices. The supply of oil has decreased from S_1 to S_3. The overall effect has been to increase price to P_3 as shown in the diagram.

8/8 marks

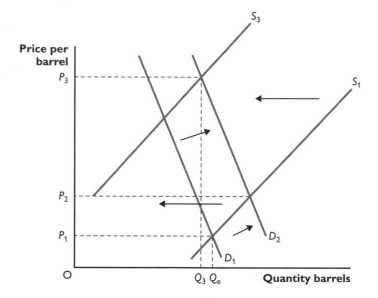

A sound answer. The candidate explains the demand and supply factors causing oil prices to rise. The demand and supply curves are shifted correctly, showing the original and new equilibrium positions. This candidate would score 4/4 marks for explanation and 4/4 marks for the diagram.

(ii) The soaring price of oil has increased the revenue and profits for oil producers, especially in the Middle East, and they have now spent more money on infrastructure and buying assets in the West. They are much better off and oil revenues are now $750 billion per year. **2/6 marks**

The answer is too brief and lacks development, especially evaluation. One way to evaluate is to consider the magnitude of the increase in oil revenues — this is likely to be huge. The candidate could also refer to the short run and long run here. There is a possibility of oil prices reaching $200 a barrel in the future and this could further increase revenue, depending on elasticity of demand. Another evaluation point could be to consider whether such high oil prices will lead to the global recession referred to in Extract 1. This candidate would receive 2/4 marks for knowledge and application and 0/2 marks for evaluation.

(b) Petrol prices have risen at a lower rate than oil prices. For example, petrol has risen by 25% and oil by 300% over the past 4 years. The main reason for this is shown in Figure 1 which shows how the price of a litre of petrol is made up. Only 32.6 pence is made up of producing petrol from oil. The oil price is probably even lower than 32.6 pence since it has to be processed into petrol. There are other costs involved in doing this, such as having the equipment and plant in place to make petrol.

A second reason is due to taxation. There is an excise duty tax of 50.35 pence and VAT of 16.07 pence per litre of petrol. Consequently, large increases in oil prices will lead to relatively lower increases in petrol prices.   **6/6 marks**

The candidate does enough to achieve full marks by recognising that petrol has other input costs than just oil. There are costs involved in producing petrol, such as retail and distribution. Also, the candidate refers to the significance of taxation. The candidate would score 4/4 marks for identifying and explaining and 2/2 marks for evaluation.

(c) An indirect tax on oil has the effect of shifting supply inwards from S_1 to S_2 on the diagram. This includes both a specific tax (50.35 pence) and an *ad valorem* tax (16.07 pence) per litre. Overall there is a pivotal shift in the supply curve. The new price is P_2 and output falls to Q_2. The tax area is shown by XYP_2W.   **5/10 marks**

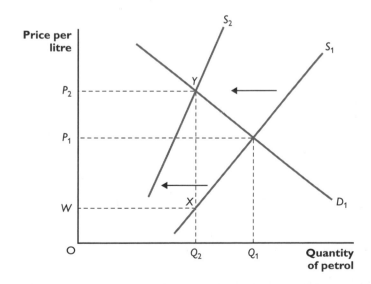

▣ The candidate achieves 5 marks for a diagram and explanation of the rising price of petrol and falling output. However, no evaluation marks are gained. Evaluation could include a discussion of petrol being an essential good and so demand would be more price inelastic. Reference to the incidence of taxation between consumers and producers would also be useful. Discussion could also include the impact of a tax on company profits and revenues. Also, would it lead to unemployment in the market or have knock-on effects in other markets? This candidate would receive 5/6 application and analysis marks and 0/4 evaluation marks.

(d) Government failure occurs if government intervention leads to a net welfare loss in a market. It is where the government causes an inefficient allocation of resources. It is a government failure since the proportion of the petrol price which comprises tax is very high at 61.6%. This seems unfair to motorists and it may cause further disruption if it leads to similar protests to those in 2000. It also means UK firms are less competitive in transporting goods if the tax is higher than in other countries. Extract 2 mentions how gas, electricity and food have all become more expensive too. It is also unfair since poorer motorists will be unable to use their car simply because it is too expensive. Better-off motorists will not be affected so much. **5/10 marks**

▣ The candidate accurately defines government failure for 2 marks and then analyses how it arises, adding value to the answer for a further 3 marks. However, the answer is one sided and so could be improved by exploring the alternative view, which would guarantee the evaluation marks. For example, the government intervenes in the first place to correct a market failure: namely, the pollution from petrol which the price mechanism ignores. The candidate could have considered the external costs from petrol such as air pollution. Also, there is noise pollution and road congestion in using motor vehicles. Discussion could also take place on what the tax revenue collected is used for. Perhaps it could be used to fund public transport or alternative forms of cleaner energy. This candidate would gain 5/6 marks for knowledge and analysis and 0/4 evaluation marks.

(e) Price elasticity of demand refers to the responsiveness of demand for a good due to a change in its price. There are several key determinants of a good, such as whether it is a luxury or necessity, the proportion of income spent on it and whether there are close substitutes. Oil is regarded as an essential good in developed economies and so demand is likely to be inelastic. This means the percentage change in demand is less than the percentage change in price. A rise in price of oil will increase revenue to oil producers and this is mentioned in the extract. The proportion of income spent on oil is relatively low in developed economies and so people may not adjust their demand by much as price rises or falls. The use of oil is also habit forming since we drive our cars all the time, so demand will remain inelastic. **4/8 marks**

🖉 The candidate explains some important determinants of price elasticity of demand and applies this to oil. However, little attempt is made to consider how elasticity might vary over time and more use of Extract 2 is required. The last paragraph suggests more substitutes are being developed along with new technology. It is likely oil will become less price inelastic over time as substitutes emerge. 4/4 marks would be awarded for knowledge and analysis and 0/4 marks for evaluation.

Total score: 30/48 = grade B

Question 3   Road traffic growth

Table 1 Transport statistics, 1995–2005 (Great Britain)

	1995	2000	2005
Licensed road vehicles (millions)	25.4	28.9	32.9
Public roads in use (km)	386,400	390,240	388,000
Railways in use (km)	15,564	15,680	15,032

Table 2 The cost of travel by motor vehicle, rail and bus (Great Britain)

	1995	2000	2005
Motoring (cars)	100	119.0	120.9
Bus fares	100	119.6	150.0
Rail fares	100	116.5	136.0
Retail price index	100	114.2	128.8

Source: *Annual Abstract of Statistics 2007*

Figure 1 Vehicle kilometres and real gross domestic product

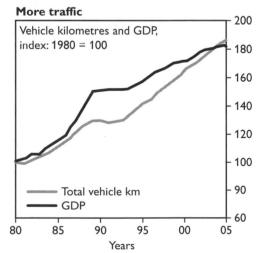

More traffic

Vehicle kilometres and GDP, index: 1980 = 100

— Total vehicle km
— GDP

Years

Source: ONS, *Travel Trends 2007*

data-response question 3

Extract 1 Increasing road congestion

Britons are more dependent on their cars than ever, driving farther to work, schools and shops, despite the government's policy of reducing the need to travel. It has contributed to a dramatic increase in road congestion. According to a government study, motorists waste up to 26 minutes for every 10 miles they travel on England's main roads, compared to journey times when traffic is flowing freely. In 2000 the government pledged to reduce congestion by 6% by 2010. But this target was abandoned in 2002 when it realised it had seriously underestimated the growing demand for motor vehicle transport.

The former minister for transport, Alistair Darling, recommended pressing ahead with a nationwide system of road pricing by charging tolls of up to £1.34 per mile on the busiest roads. He stated: 'Looking ahead we need to make tough choices. That is why I believe road pricing has an essential part to play. Make no mistake, simply building more roads cannot be the answer.'

However, road pricing is very unpopular with motorists. In 2007, more than 1.5 million people signed a petition against a nationwide road congestion charge. Many see it as another opportunity for the government to tax motorists who already pay the highest fuel duties in Europe. There are also implications for businesses such as road haulage firms, transporting goods, and motorists travelling to work. For many, bus and rail transport is not a realistic alternative to the motor car. In 2008, the election for Mayor of London saw Ken Livingstone, who introduced a congestion charge in the city, voted out of office.

(a) (i) Using examples and an appropriate diagram, distinguish between the private costs and external costs of motoring for a road haulage firm.   (6 marks)

   (ii) With reference to Tables 1 and 2 and Figure 1, examine three factors that might explain the 'dramatic increase in road congestion' between 1995 and 2005 (*Extract 1, line 3*).   (12 marks)

(b) Evaluate the case for and against the introduction of a nationwide system of road pricing.   (12 marks)

(c) Examine the likely effectiveness of the following for reducing road congestion:
   (i) A major road-building programme   (6 marks)
   (ii) An increase in subsidies for bus and rail transport   (6 marks)

(d) Discuss whether road space is a public or private good.   (6 marks)

■ ■ ■

Candidate's answer

(a) (i) Private costs are internal to an exchange which the price mechanism directly takes into account — for example, a road haulage firm would have to pay for drivers and fuel to run its lorries. External costs are negative third party effects which the price mechanism ignores — for example, road congestion and air pollution caused by lorries. Private costs and external costs added together make up social costs as shown in the diagram. **6/6 marks**

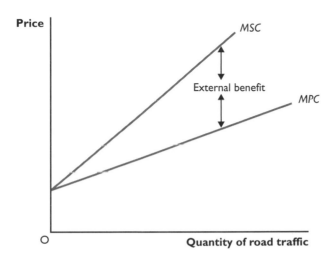

A sound answer. The candidate follows the instructions and defines both concepts, provides relevant examples and uses a diagram.

(ii) The dramatic increase in road congestion is due to the growth in motor vehicles exceeding the growth in road space over the period 1995–2005. The number of licensed motor vehicles rose from 25.4 million to 32.9 million (29.5%) while the amount of road space rose from 386,400 km to 388,000 km (0.4%). This means there are more vehicles for every kilometre of public road.

Another reason for increased congestion over this period is due to the real price of car travel falling but the real price of bus and rail travel rising. This is indicated by comparing the price of travel with the RPI rate of inflation in Table 2. Bus and rail travel are substitutes with a positive cross elasticity of demand. An increase in price of buses and trains leads to an increase in demand for car travel. **6/12 marks**

The candidate explains two reasons, using the data and economic analysis such as cross elasticity of demand. 3 + 3 marks would be awarded for this. However, one more reason is required. The candidate could have referred to the increase in real GDP over the period shown in Figure 1, making the purchase of cars and motoring more affordable, or mentioned the reduction in length of the public rail

ata-response question 3

track (which implies fewer rail services on offer). Finally, the candidate needs to offer two evaluation points: for example, discussing the extent to which rail and bus travel are substitutes for cars. In addition, discussion of the magnitude of the increase in licensed vehicles could be developed. Even prioritisation of the most important cause of traffic congestion could be made with justification. 6/8 marks for knowledge, application and analysis and 0/4 marks for evaluation would be awarded here.

(b) There are several advantages of a nationwide road pricing system. First, it will enable the government to increase the price of motoring for those who travel during peak periods and cause congestion. It is a way of making the polluter pay for the congestion and so is fair. Also it will encourage motorists to vary the time of their journeys so that they do not pay at off-peak times and reduce congestion. It will also reduce non-essential journeys by car. Road pricing will also bring in some revenue for the government to spend on reducing congestion, for example, public transport improvements. Road pricing is desirable since it reduces other forms of external costs such as air and noise pollution. It will reduce global warming.

The disadvantage of road pricing is that it is unpopular with motorists as shown by the number of people signing a petition. It increases the cost of motoring and people are objecting to this. **6/12 marks**

The answer is imbalanced, concentrating mainly on the advantages of road pricing, but offering very little on the disadvantages. Consequently, the candidate does not gain much in terms of evaluation (developing both sides of an argument, as instructed in the question). Disadvantages could include the impact on low-income motorists, the costs of implementing the scheme, privacy issues and whether motorists will find alternative minor roads not subject to the charge. The answer also lacks caution throughout. Economics is an imperfect social science and so it is more appropriate to state that certain things 'may' or 'could' happen rather than will happen. This candidate would receive 5/8 marks for knowledge and analysis and 1/4 marks for evaluation.

(c) (i) A major road building programme will not reduce traffic congestion since it can never keep up with the growth in motor vehicles. This is shown in Table 1; between 1995 and 2005, public roads increased by 0.4% but motor vehicles by 29.5%. Roads are also expensive to build and involve lengthy planning inquiries. The time taken to build makes congestion worse in the short run. However, if the road building focuses on areas which suffer from great traffic congestion, then it will have some positive effect. Main areas of road conges-tion include the M1, M6 and M25 motorways. But then in the long run, it will increase the number of motorists using the roads until there is lots of conges-tion again. **6/6 marks**

A sound answer. The candidate makes use of the data in Table 1 and considers both views in investigating the effectiveness of more road building. The candidate still needs to be more cautious in making statements but gets away with it here and would receive 3/3 marks for knowledge and application and 3/3 marks for evaluation.

(ii) Increased subsidies to bus and rail transport will not help since motorists do not want to use them. They are inconvenient since people still have to get to a bus stop or rail station. Also, the frequency of buses and trains is poor. Table 2 shows that they are expensive too. **2/6 marks**

✐ The answer is too brief and lacks economic analysis. Analysis of a subsidy diagram would be helpful. Also the candidate could evaluate by discussing the size of the subsidy and how it might improve the frequency of buses and trains. Furthermore, a subsidy should reduce fares and so make it more attractive for motorists to use. This candidate would receive 2/3 marks for knowledge and application, but 0/3 marks for evaluation.

(d) Road space is a public good since anyone can use it. Roads are built by the government for motorists to use. If they were run by private firms who charge for using the roads they would become private goods. **2/6 marks**

✐ The answer is too brief. It could be improved through defining key terms such as private and public goods. This would also help direct the candidate's answer. An evaluative point includes the idea that road space is a quasi-public good. It displays characteristics of non-rivalry and non-excludability at off peak times and so is like a public good. However, during peak-times motorists compete for road space and it becomes a private good. Also, to make use of road space the individual needs to have a motor vehicle, otherwise one cannot use it. This answer would only receive 2/4 marks for knowledge and application and 0/2 marks for evaluation.

Total score: 28/48 = grade C

Question 4   UK healthcare provision

Table 1 Number of NHS staff by occupation, 1997–2007

Occupation	1997	2007	% increase
Doctors and consultants	89,619	128,210	43.0
Nurses	318,856	399,597	25.3
Scientific and technical staff	96,298	136,976	42.3
Managers	22,173	36,499	64.6
Other support staff	531,740	629,827	18.4
Total	**1,058,686**	**1,331.109**	**25.7**

Source: ONS 2007

d ata-response question 4

Figure 1 Average waiting times for treatment in the NHS

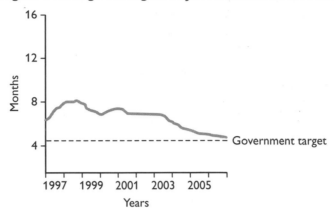

Source: ONS 2007

Figure 2 NHS hospital beds

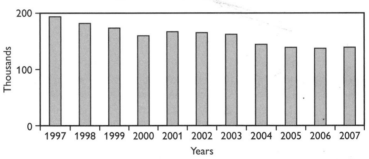

Source: ONS 2007

Extract 1 Growing pressures on the NHS

The NHS is the largest employer in Europe. It deals with over 1 million patients every 36 hours. Between 1997 and 2007 government spending on the NHS increased from £41 billion to £105 billion. It now comprises 8% of GDP.

The increase in NHS spending reflects rising demand and cost pressures: for example, changes in the size and age structure of the population and public expectations over standards. Over 100 new hospitals have been built since 1997 along with employment of extra staff.

However, not all the money seems to have been well spent. Staff salaries have soared, while productivity has fallen by 10% in terms of the number of patients each doctor and consultant treats. This fall in productivity is disputed by staff, who point to improvements in the quality of treatment.

The NHS provides free healthcare at the point of use. However, this has created an excess demand for treatment, leading to long waiting lists.

(a) (i) Calculate the percentage increase in government spending on the   (2 marks)
NHS between 1997 and 2007. (*Extract 1, lines 2–3*)

  (ii) Assess three likely causes of this increase in government   (10 marks)
expenditure on the NHS.

(b) Discuss the significance of opportunity cost to the increase in   (6 marks)
government spending on the NHS.

(c) With reference to the information provided, discuss whether the   (10 marks)
increased funding of the NHS has improved the quality of healthcare
provision.

(d) Assess the importance of private and external benefits arising from   (12 marks)
the consumption of healthcare. Illustrate your answer with an
appropriate diagram.

(e) Discuss the extent to which 'free healthcare at the point of use' has   (8 marks)
created an excess demand for treatment in the NHS. Use a supply
and demand diagram in your answer.

■ ■ ■

Candidate's answer

(a) (i) $\dfrac{(105 - 41)}{41} \times 100 = 156\%$ **2/2 marks**

🄴 Sound answer. Remember to show your calculations.

  (ii) The increase in government spending could be due to population changes in
the UK. There is an ageing population which means that as people get older
they are more prone to illness and so make greater use of doctors and hospitals. There has also been an increase in the population over recent years due
to immigration from central and eastern Europe. A second cause could be
due to new diseases and the development of medical knowledge which has
led to more expensive treatments being made available. A third possible cause
could be due to the increased number of factor inputs — for example, 100
new hospitals and many more doctors and nurses employed. All this costs
money which has to be paid for by the government.   **6/10 marks**

🄴 The candidate has made effective use of the pointers in the information provided.
However, the answer lacks evaluation: for example, prioritising between the
causes of growth in spending on the NHS and the significance of the time period.
One might discuss whether the figures are in nominal or real terms, although this
cannot account for the sheer magnitude of growth. This answer would receive
6/6 marks for application and analysis and 0/4 marks for evaluation.

data-response question 4

(b) Opportunity cost refers to the value of the next best alternative foregone. The rise in government spending on the NHS has an opportunity cost since the funds could have been spent on education or defence instead. Similarly, the government could have reduced the size of its debts or even cut taxation.   **4/6 marks**

> 🖉 A good answer. The candidate defines opportunity cost and then explores possible alternative uses of the funds. However, no evaluation is offered, such as a discussion of the implications of selecting one choice over another. For example, the candidate could have explored the impact the spending has had on economic growth and living standards in the long term compared with spending the money elsewhere. This answer would therefore receive 4/4 for knowledge and application, but 0/2 for evaluation.

(c) Increased funding of the NHS has definitely improved the quality of healthcare. The magnitude of the increase in spending (156%) has ensured this. However, it would be useful to know whether these figures are in real or nominal terms. Nevertheless, inflation has been relatively low over the past ten years, so even if the figures are in nominal terms, they are still impressive. Table 1 shows a 43% increase in the number of doctors and a 25.3% increase in nurses. This probably helped to reduce waiting times shown in Figure 1.

However, the number of hospital beds has fallen from nearly 200,000 to around 130,000 over the ten years. This suggests the quantity of healthcare has reduced. Yet we are told that the NHS treats more than 1 million people every 36 hours. To make a better evaluation we need to know what the extra government funding has been spent on. If most of it has been on staff salaries then the quality of provision may not be so good. On the other hand, higher salaries could lead to a more motivated and productive workforce. Table 1 shows a bigger rate of increase in health managers than doctors and nurses, but it could lead to better use of the vast funds available.

To conclude, it is very difficult to measure the quality of healthcare provision. For example, the 10% decrease in productivity could simply mean more time and care is being spent treating each patient. We need further information on things like success rates from different treatments.   **10/10 marks**

> 🖉 A sound answer. The candidate makes effective use of the data and offers lots of analysis and evaluation. A critical approach has been taken to the data which is valid in this case and so this answer would receive 6/6 marks for knowledge, application and analysis and 4/4 marks for evaluation.

(d) Private benefits refer to the benefits internal to an exchange. They include the benefits in terms of salaries to staff employed and the revenues gained by firms supplying healthcare services — for example, medicines and X-ray scanning equipment. Private benefits from healthcare are very important to the economy since it is a direct source of income and employment to thousands of people.

External benefits refer to third party benefits outside of a market transaction. They include a healthier workforce, which means people take less time off work for illness and so are more productive. Furthermore, the government may experience improved finances since tax revenue should rise and spending on unemployment and disability benefits should fall. There is also a reduction in the spread of contagious diseases, since most people receive free vaccinations. This should increase the life expectancy of the general population and raise the supply of labour available for firms.

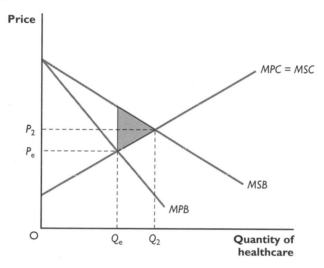

The diagram shows private, external and social benefits. It also reveals the area of welfare gain if healthcare provision is raised to the social optimum position of Q_2, where $MSB = MSC$. If left to the market, MSB would exceed MSC at output Q_e and so it is not the best position for society. It appears that the external benefits to be gained are so important as to make it worthwhile for the government to spend £111 billion and fund this through taxation rather than leave it to the private sector.   **10/12 marks**

🖉 A sound answer. The candidate accurately defines private and external benefits and then develops relevant explanation and examples for 6/6 marks. Two evaluation points are made by suggesting that the external benefits gained are important enough for the government to fund through taxation and by discussion of the area of welfare gain, which would receive 4/6 evaluation marks.

(e) Free healthcare at the point of use has created an excess demand. This is where demand exceeds supply at the set price, in this case zero. This is shown in the diagram (overleaf) as the quantity Q_eQ_2. Supply of healthcare is a vertical line to represent the fixed budget for the NHS.   **4/8 marks**

data-response question 4

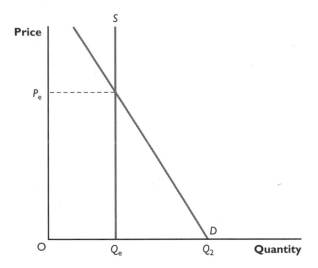

A good answer but a little brief. The candidate could extend the explanation by showing how excess demand would be eliminated in a free market by price rising to P_e and demand contracting to Q_e. An evaluative comment is also required: for example, discussion of the magnitude of the excess demand. The candidate could make reference to NHS waiting lists. Some discussion of the distinction between a 'want' and 'effective demand' could also be regarded as evaluation here. People may need health treatment but simply cannot afford it. 4/6 marks would be awarded for application and analysis and 0/2 marks for evaluation.

Total score: 36/48 = grade A–